RESCUING
RETIREMENT

RESCUING RETIREMENT

TERESA GHILARDUCCI
AND TONY JAMES

FOREWORD BY TIMOTHY GEITHNER

COLUMBIA UNIVERSITY PRESS | NEW YORK

Columbia University Press
Publishers Since 1893
New York   Chichester, West Sussex
cup.columbia.edu
Copyright © 2018 Teresa Ghilarducci and Hamilton E. James
All rights reserved

Library of Congress Cataloging-in-Publication Data
Names: Ghilarducci, Teresa, author. | James, Tony, 1951- author.
Title: Rescuing retirement / Teresa Ghilarducci and Tony James.
Description: 1 Edition. | New York : Columbia University Press, [2018] |
Includes bibliographical references and index.
Identifiers: LCCN 2017035932 (print) | LCCN 2017037759 (ebook)
| ISBN 9780231546270 | ISBN 9780231185646 (alk. paper)
Subjects: LCSH: Retirement income—United States—Planning. |
Retirement—United States—Planning.
Classification: LCC HG179 (ebook) | LCC HG179 .G4734 2018 (print) |
DDC 332.024/01450973—dc23
LC record available at https://lccn.loc.gov/2017035932

Cover design: Lydia Fine
Cover photograph: Peter Dazeley ©GettyImages

To our mothers, Waleska James and Marion Ghilarducci, for their support for us and their generosity of spirit toward the world at large.

To the next generation, especially Joseph Ghilarducci O'Rourke and Genevieve McGahey, and Meredith, Becky, and Ham James.

And to all the retirees of tomorrow, who are entitled to retire with dignity.

Our plan would guarantee millions of Americans safe and secure retirements that would benefit them, their families, and the nation's economy.

—Teresa Ghilarducci and Hamilton E. James.
"A Smarter Plan to Make Retirement Savings Last,"
New York Times, January 1, 2016

CONTENTS

CONTENTS

FOREWORD

TIMOTHY GEITHNER

The United States faces a discouraging mix of long-term economic challenges and the diminished capacity of the political system to deliver a framework of incentives and investments that can address these challenges.

Among these challenges, the lack of retirement security is one of the most daunting. As Teresa Ghilarducci and Tony James write, this is a problem for the vast majority of working Americans. It won't go away on its own. Without a substantial change in individual savings and investing behavior, we face a future with tens of millions of elderly poor.

Americans typically save a relatively small portion of their income. The savings rate moved a bit higher after the trauma of the financial crisis of 2008, but it remains low. A large majority of Americans do not have a financial cushion adequate to cover their immediate needs, much less their needs in the decades they will live after they retire.

Neither the behavior of individuals nor economic policy has adapted to a world in which people are living longer, health care costs are expensive and rising, median income growth is slower, and expected returns on financial assets are lower. With the end of an employer-based defined-contribution system and with changes in the health care system, we have shifted a lot of economic risk to the individual, but individuals are having a hard time adapting to that new reality.

Many other economies have enacted fundamental reforms of their pension systems, but our system remains burdened by some fundamental shortcomings. We have an elaborate set of expensive tax preferences that appear to have little effect on encouraging savings and whose benefits go disproportionately to the relatively fortunate. The savings products that have succeeded the defined-benefit plans of the past are designed in ways that enable the worst instincts of individual investors, without giving them access to the investment models that allow them to gain some of the benefits of a long-term investment horizon.

Unsustainable long-term deficits mean that individuals have to contemplate a future with higher taxes and lower benefits. Individuals will have to pay more for retirement and more for health care during retirement. The longer-term constraints on our fiscal resources mean we have to be careful how we allocate those benefits today, including through the tax code and its provisions designed to encourage savings.

Teresa Ghilarducci and Tony James make a powerful case for reform, and they have designed a system better than what we have today that would complement, not substitute for, Social Security. Their proposal combines the best features of the reforms adopted in other countries, without adding an unrealistic and unaffordable commitment of future tax resources. They approach the challenge without ideological bias, guided by a refreshingly pragmatic focus on what the evidence suggests is likely to work.

ACKNOWLEDGMENTS

First and foremost, we thank Will Pollock for his invaluable research, writing, and editing throughout this process. We also thank Christine Anderson and Peter Rose for their enthusiastic support and encouragement. Pete Peterson is an inspiration who proves that a lone voice can make a difference, and that business leaders bear an obligation to help solve society's problems. Neera Tanden got this all started by asking us to do a policy speech in Washington, D.C. around a new big idea.

Jeffrey Nussbaum, Michael Flynn, and Adam Talbot lent their policy expertise and formidable writing skills to refine the plan. Teresa's New School colleagues, Rick McGahey, Will Milberg, David VanZandt, Bridget Fisher, and Tony Webb, are admirably determined and committed to advance a constructive national plan for retirement security. Bridget was indispensable in communicating this book's ideas to the media and to stakeholders, and Tony lent his expertise as an economist to confirm many of our numbers.

Throughout this process, we have been fortunate to meet and speak with leading economists—including Erskine Bowles, Austan Goolsbee, Glenn Hubbard, Alan Krueger, Alicia Munnell, Larry Summers, Timothy Geithner, and Robert Rubin—and with elected officials from across the political spectrum. Republicans and Democrats alike have expressed determination to find common ground to solve the retirement crisis. We are profoundly grateful for their commitment to this cause.

We also want to recognize the countless Americans struggling to do the right thing in a broken system: employers who do all they can to provide retirement savings support for their staff, and employees who work more hours per week, more weeks per year, and more years per lifetime than workers in most wealthy nations. These dedicated men and women deserve a better retirement system, one in which their money works as hard as they do to secure their standard of living for the full span of their lives.

RESCUING
RETIREMENT

1

SOCIETY'S RETIREMENT CRISIS

" **M**y retirement plan," Robert Hiltonsmith told PBS's *Frontline*, "is 'fingers crossed and pray,' basically. Yeah, win the lottery.... The truth is, [I'm] just going to have to find a way to save way more than you should have to."[1]

An economist in his mid-thirties, Robert's plight captures much of what is wrong with the U.S. retirement system. Given his promising career and relative youth, he should have all the tools he needs to plan for a comfortable retirement. But his outlook could not be more pessimistic—or revealing.

A Society of Actuaries survey showed that a majority of Americans believe retirement benefits should provide a guaranteed amount monthly during retirement no matter how long they live.[2] But today, our retirement system is so hopelessly broken—and so deeply confusing—that even Americans with well-paying, full-time jobs their entire adult lives are hard-pressed to guarantee a comfortable and secure future.

Tens of millions of lower-income workers face an even more daunting challenge. Without significant savings, they must try to continue working to the end of their lives, knowing that a single health crisis, accident, or layoff could spiral them into poverty.

Retirement is a significant source of stress in people's lives (figure 1.1).

Our nation stands at a watershed moment. More Americans than ever are approaching retirement with inadequate savings. Their numbers are poised to grow dramatically in coming years because we are both saving less and living longer. Further aggravating this problem is that too many people—56 percent of men and 64 percent of women—unwisely claim Social Security before full retirement age.[3]

Since 1980, the number of Americans making it into their nineties has tripled. Today's retirees will need their

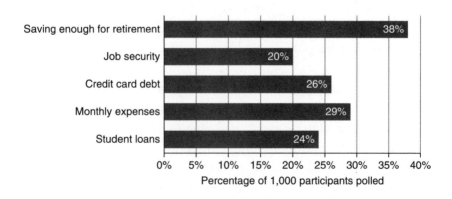

Figure 1.1 Young workers say they're worried about retirement. (Answers to the question "What is a 'significant source of stress' in your life?").

Source: Schwab Retirement Plan Services, Inc. (August 2016) 401(k) Participant Survey.

savings to last longer than ever.[4] As life expectancies rise, the prevailing retirement income plans—mostly 401(k)s and Individual Retirement Accounts (IRAs)—are proving less and less adequate. Our patchwork system leaves too many people with paltry savings and anemic investment returns.

The U.S. experiment with 401(k)s and IRAs, launched in the 1980s, has failed miserably to deliver on its promises. Predatory fees, low returns, leakages, lump-sum payouts—all have served to discourage or inhibit workers from accumulating enough for retirement. Here is the hard reality: more than half of working people nearing retirement today won't have enough to maintain their standard of living.[5] Among Americans between forty and fifty-five, the median retirement account balance is $14,500[6]—less than 4 percent of the $375,000 the median-income worker will need in savings.[7]

For the next generations of retirees—including today's young people—the challenges will be greater still. For the past forty years, America's median household income has stagnated; ditto for entry-level wages. In real terms, our minimum wage has regressed to where it was in the 1940s, a time when most workers were eligible for true pensions.

Meanwhile, health care costs are rising two to three times faster than income; rent and child care expenses are escalating; and outstanding student loan debt has tripled over the last decade to more than $1 trillion. When we compare the last half-century to the next fifty years, productivity and economic growth rates are projected to drop by half. Meanwhile, ultra-low-interest rates are depressing returns on any savings we somehow manage to put aside.

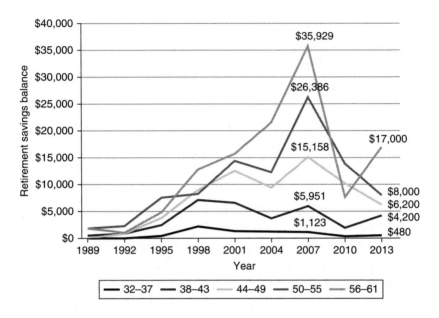

Figure 1.2 Median retirement account savings of families by age, 1989–2013 (2013 dollars).

When it comes to retirement savings, across all age groups, the United States is acutely behind where it needs to be (figure 1.2).

Given this stark reality, it is little wonder that a 2015 survey found that 86 percent of Americans believe "the nation faces a retirement crisis."[8]

Based on current trends, we will soon be facing rates of elder poverty unseen since the Great Depression. Of the 18 million workers between ages fifty-five and sixty-four in 2012, 4.3 million were projected to be poor or near-poor when they turn sixty-five,[9] including 2.6 million who were part of the middle class before reaching retirement age.

Today, 15 million elderly people spend less than twelve dollars per day for food. By 2035, nearly 20 million retirees will be living in poverty or near-poverty. By 2050, that number will reach 25 million (figure 1.3).

As the U.S. population continues to simultaneously grow and gray, and traditional pensions become relics of the past, elderly people living in deprivation will become a progressively greater share of the population. This wave of older poor Americans will strain our social safety net programs, from the Supplemental Nutrition Assistance Program (SNAP) to Medicaid. It will devastate federal, state, and local budgets.

Figure 1.3

Source: T. Ghilarducci and Z. Knauss. (2015) "More Middle Class Workers Will Be Poor Retirees." Schwartz Center for Economic Policy Analysis and Department of Economics. The New School for Social Research. Policy Note Series.

Left unaddressed, poverty among the elderly could drive up federal income tax rates by ten percentage points. The expenses of poor or near-poor older Americans will inevitably be passed on to other citizens, from higher Medicaid entitlements (for nursing homes and assisted living costs) to the taxpayer burden from a spike in homelessness.

It may be tempting to fault the savers for this sad state of affairs, but it is wrong to blame the victim. Here is the hard truth: existing tools make it impossible for most people to afford to save enough for retirement, and employers are not bridging the gap. People could try to delay retiring, but for various reasons that isn't always the worker's choice to make. Even those with significant savings to invest commonly see subpar returns, due in large part to lack of financial literacy and an industry short on reliable advice. Financial advisors, whose fees to their clients cost savers an estimated $17 billion per year, often guide them into trouble.[10]

It is not individual workers who are to blame for our retirement crisis. Nor is it their employers. It is the fault of a haphazard, ramshackle system.

We cannot educate people out of this crisis. Given the reality on the ground, the most sophisticated among us would be hard-pressed to master the complex machinery of "personal finance." Yet instead of focusing on reforms to fix our train wreck of a retirement system, our policy makers are distracted by campaigns for partial stop-gap measures. As lawmakers grapple with payday loans and usurious credit card interest rates, retirement security goes by the boards. The World Economic Forum (WEF) estimates that the United States had

A SIMPLIFIED APPROACH TO PROVIDING RETIREMENT SECURITY

1. **Every worker owns a portable retirement saving account.** However long they work before retirement, employees maintain total control over a government guaranteed account. It is funded by a minimum 3 percent of the employee's salary—half contributed by the worker, half by the employer. A tax credit fully subsidizes the employee's share for all those earning under the median income and defrays the cost for everyone else. (We talk more about this later.)
2. **Savings are pooled and invested to achieve higher returns.** Workers select a GRA pension manager who invests in relatively high-return, well-diversified strategies. People can change managers annually. Pension managers have a fiduciary duty to GRA holders and provide a layer of protection between them and Wall Street.
3. **Upon retirement, the account is annuitized** to provide consistent, government guaranteed income until death.

a $28 trillion retirement savings gap in 2015—the largest in the world. By 2050, they project this will grow to $137 trillion. This is almost a $3 trillion annual increase—five times the annual U.S. defense budget.[11]

In sum, our country is facing an across-the-board retirement savings gap (Figure 1.4). Americans of almost all ages and income levels face nearly insurmountable obstacles to building a strong retirement foundation. One way or another, this crisis will affect us all in the years to come.

$290,000

$14,500

Average retirement
savings

Retirement savings
needed

Figure 1.4

Sources: Center for American Progress (2015) "The Reality of the Retirement Crisis." Aon Hewitt (2012) "Retirement Income Adequacy at Large Companies: The Real Deal."

A BETTER WAY FORWARD

There's a better way forward for our country. It is a journey we can start today, drawing on straightforward, proven ideas.

It's a way to ensure every full-time worker can save enough to guarantee his or her standard of living in retirement.
A way to save for retirement with a tool that delivers a higher and safer rate of return than the typical 401(k) or IRA.
A way to address a national crisis without adding a dime to the deficit or creating any new government infrastructure.

In this book, we have designed a retirement system that meets all of these specifications and delivers a retirement plan to 85 million Americans that don't have one today. And our solution is simpler than you might think. It is called a Guaranteed Retirement Account, or GRA.

What the GRA Is

Pragmatism, Not Politics

The GRA is a pragmatic way to ensure that all workers can save enough to retire. The plan moves our retirement system from an inefficient hodgepodge to a unified, sustainable, high-performing, pro-growth framework for failsafe retirement. Our plan is built for bipartisanship, drawing on the best ideas from both parties.

(continued)

A Universal Retirement Solution

GRAs offer everyone, from Uber drivers to CEOs, their own fully portable accounts. Under our plan, 85 million Americans who currently do not have a retirement plan would receive one.

A Helping Hand (Not a Handout)

The GRA is a personal retirement savings vehicle, not a government entitlement. It delivers via individually owned accounts and uses existing government infrastructure.

A Plan That Keeps You in Control

Our plan is built on convenience, personal choice, private ownership, and effective investment. You accumulate your money in your own account. If you die before retirement, your savings are passed on to your heirs.

Security for Life

A GRA represents lifelong retirement security. Each account is converted into a government paid annuity that assures postretirement income and a set standard of living as long as the retiree lives.

A Mandated Gift

Although mandatory, a GRA is essentially cost-free for employees earning less than the U.S. median salary. With an annual matching $600 tax credit for all workers contributing to their GRAs, households earning up to $40,000 per year have their savings fully reimbursed. Higher-earning individuals also receive this $600 tax credit and deduct the balance of their 1.5 percent contribution from their taxes.

What the Retirement Savings Plan Is Not

Not Another Form of Social Security

This is your own money in your own account, outside the government's purview. Each individual gets an annuity with personally accumulated retirement savings. What's more, the plan leaves Social Security unburdened.

Not Another New Government Bureaucracy

GRAs use existing government infrastructure to deliver annuity payments, and nothing more. Individuals contribute to a pooled trust managed by a pension manager of their choosing. Returns are higher and administrative fees are lower than in individually directed accounts. Account-holders decide when to retire and convert their savings into lifelong income.

Not a Source of New Taxes or a Larger Deficit

The plan's tax credits are paid in full by redistributing existing government subsidies from the wealthiest Americans to the entire taxpaying population. In addition, by tackling the retirement crisis head-on, the plan creates future government savings.

Our plan requires all U.S. workers to contribute alongside their employers into an account wholly owned and controlled by the worker him- or herself.[12] Because GRA savings are invested by regulated professionals into a diversified portfolio of high-performing assets, they can grow substantially over time. The accounts are pooled, so they leverage rock-bottom fees and other economies of scale. A principal protection guarantee buffers savers against economic and market meltdowns.

GRAs are fully portable, with balances unaffected by moves to different employers or states. And GRAs are immune to the erosion that is endemic to 401(k)s; employees are barred from withdrawing their money before they stop working. Upon retirement, GRAs produce consistent income, month to month and year to year, ensuring people's quality of life by filling the gap between Social Security and the cost of living. They provide a reliable pension equivalent, paying out a steady stream of income over the entirety of the worker's life—the biggest single missing piece in today's defined-contribution plans.

A healthy and secure retirement system has three components. The first is a Social Security system, which keeps existing benefits secure. The second is a Medicare system, which guarantees health care to all retirees. And the third is a pension-style retirement income delivered by our plan. The GRA represents the critical missing step toward fixing our broken retirement system.

GRAs are not a replacement for Social Security, an essential safety net that may soon need shoring up. Our plan supplements Social Security. It is an alternate approach that empowers workers to save enough for retirement when Social Security falls short.

Our GRA plan leverages the best practices of Canada, Australia, and other countries that have successfully secured retirement for their populations. GRAs enhance both individual savings and lifetime retirement benefits, and advances an idea both political parties can support: government-backed accounts under individual control that do not swell the budget, raise taxes, or create new government bureaucracy.

We know there is demand for a solution to our coming retirement crisis. The vast majority of Americans want policy makers to address this challenge. In national focus groups conducted across different regions and demographics, our plan received overwhelming support. Overall, 71 percent of participants supported our policy recommendations for a national retirement system so simple it could be enacted tomorrow.

All Americans stand to benefit from a smart, fiscally sound retirement system—one that is built on personal responsibility, facilitates personal savings, harnesses the benefits of economic growth for all, and guarantees that full-time workers will be secure in their retirement. That's why we wrote this book.

* * *

This proposal is the product of an unlikely pairing.

Tony is the president and chief operating officer of one of the world's leading investment firms. He has seen firsthand how our current retirement system performs in the market—and how, by design, Americans' savings are invested in ways that consistently underdeliver. This squandered return has profound repercussions. It leaves the vast majority of retired senior citizens without enough retirement savings to support themselves.

Teresa is a leading expert in retirement economics. She has spent decades chronicling the impact on the shift in U.S. retirement planning from employers to employees, most of whom are unprepared for the task. Her research has revealed why so many Americans wind up retiring in poverty even after doing their utmost to save for the future.

Together, we share the belief that our nation needs to change course—and soon—to avoid a retirement catastrophe. This book shows how a Guaranteed Retirement Account plan solves a critical problem facing the vast majority of Americans. We also cite relevant case studies and consider prospects for legislative action.

First, though, let's explore how our current retirement system has set the country on such a perilous path.

2

HOW WE GOT HERE

America's Broken Retirement System

The first step toward solving America's retirement crisis is to recognize that our existing national "system" is an inefficient, randomly assembled jumble. Not so long ago, nearly half of all workers counted on a guaranteed pension from their employers. As recently as 1979, half of all private sector workers with retirement plans had traditional, employer-administered pensions.[1]

Although pensions have shortcomings,[2] defined-benefit plans have long been preferred by anyone seeking stable retirement income. Today, however, only 15 percent of the U.S. workforce (mostly government workers and public school teachers) has access to a traditional pension. Beginning in the 1980s, most private employers shifted to "defined-contribution" plans such as 401(k)s, which cost companies less and shift funding risk from companies to employees. Roughly half of private sector workers (53% in 2016) either lack access to *any* plan or do not participate in one.

In other words, an employer-backed retirement guarantee has been replaced by an ill-designed system where savers sink or swim. U.S. workers are cobbling together their own retirement plans without the knowledge, tools, or marketplace leverage to do so effectively. Many workers turn to options such as Keogh plans (tax-deferred retirement vehicles for small businesses or the self-employed). Similar to 401(k)s, these defined-contribution plans provide no guaranteed return once the individual retires. Unlike 401(k)s, they offer neither employer contributions nor appropriate investment vehicles and annuity options.

Social Security provides a base of retirement security, but it was designed to be a modest social insurance program, not the basis for a middle-class lifestyle. Today's average monthly Social Security benefit is $1,300, insufficient to meet baseline needs for most retirees.[3] Yet for more than one-third of recipients, the program currently provides more than 90 percent of their income. For 24 percent of retirees, Social Security is their *only* source of income.

The vast majority of American workers are cobbling together their own retirement plans without the knowledge, tools, or marketplace leverage to do so effectively.

Research shows that even participants in defined-contribution plans fail to consistently save or efficiently invest. It is important to remember that the 401(k)—now the primary U.S. retirement vehicle—was never intended to be an omnibus solution.[4] It emerged largely by accident over the past three decades, starting as a fallback, then gaining momentum as the primary retirement vehicle as employers eliminated defined-benefit plans.[5]

One recent Federal Reserve survey of people whose employers offer a retirement plan but who do not participate shows that 27 percent of them say they cannot afford to save any money. Another 18 percent are too confused by their choices, 18 percent more are not eligible to participate at all, and another 16 percent have not "gotten around" to signing up.

—Ron Lieber, "Getting a Reverse Mortgage, but Not from a Celebrity," *New York Times*, June 10, 2016.

THE ACCIDENTAL BIRTH— AND GROWTH—OF THE 401(K)

In 1980, Ted Benna, a benefits consultant, was assigned to create a savings program for his employer. Thinking logically, he consulted a copy of the Internal Revenue Code. Paging through it, he found an obscure provision granting employers a special tax status for encouraging workers to save for retirement. He took the idea and ran with it.

"Well, how about adding a match, an additional incentive?" Benna recalled thinking at the time. "Immediately, I jumped to 'Wow, this is a big deal!'" The section of the tax code? Section 401(k).[6]

Benna was right; his discovery was a big deal. Employers quickly realized that it shifted the burden and risk from themselves to their employees. Workers did not fully appreciate what they were losing, and 401(k)s took off. In 1985, there were 30,000 401(k) plans in existence. Today, there are 638,000 plans.[7]

Not bad for a glorified tax loophole, but here is the catch: for most savers, it does not work. Benna himself has assailed the 401(k) as overwhelmingly complex—a "monster"—for any worker without a background in finance and investing. "I knew it was going to be big," he said, "but I was certainly not anticipating that it would be the primary way that people would be accumulating money for retirement 30 plus years later."[8]

Direct-contribution savings vehicles have fundamental weaknesses, starting with the fact that they are voluntary. For 401(k)s to be effective, annual contributions must be made consistently throughout a worker's career, beginning in the individual's mid-twenties. In practice, most people make contributions erratically—a serious problem. Even when contributions are made with regularity and matched by the employer, 401(k)s tend to earn subpar returns due to poor investment strategies and high administrative expenses.

In brief, our retirement crisis is the result of a disastrous thirty-five-year experiment with do-it-yourself 401(k)s. This confusing, burdensome system undermines workers' efforts to accumulate adequate retirement assets. It fails to invest savings effectively. Costs are high. Perhaps most damning, no one's 401(k) is assured to last long enough in retirement. Typical participants simply will be unable to maintain their standard of living after they stop working.

401(K) PLANS HAVE NOT EXPANDED COVERAGE

Expanding Social Security could shore up those at the bottom, but middle-class and more affluent individuals need another layer of retirement income to maintain their preretirement lifestyles. No nation has ever successfully paid for middle-class retirement with an unfunded, strictly pay-as-you-go system (see Greece) or a pure 401(k) system (see Chile). The U.S. Social Security system, supplemented by workplace pensions, once offered retirement security for the middle class and narrowed the retirement wealth gap. But the swing to 401(k)s has eroded that essential second tier of savings. It has made retirement security a luxury for a privileged few.

To make matters worse, the 401(k) system has failed in its promise to provide widespread coverage. In 1980, 62 percent of full-time employees between twenty-five and sixty-four were covered by a workplace retirement plan. In 2015, only half of this group was covered (figure 2.1). In a number of states, covered workers represent a distinct minority, including Alabama (39 percent), Oklahoma (40 percent), and South Carolina (40 percent). See appendix C for a full list of retirement plan coverage rates by state.[9]

A credible retirement savings system ensures an accumulation of savings, safeguards the money, invests it efficiently, and pays out steadily throughout the individual's retired life. The 401(k) model fails on all four counts:

- When less than half the population is covered, most employees by definition will be unable to save sufficiently.

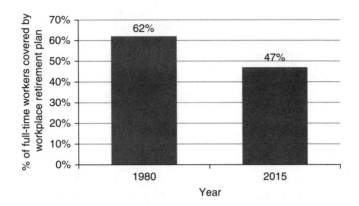

Figure 2.1 Retirement plan coverage has fallen since 401(k)s were established.

Source: Author's Calculation using the Annual Social and Economic Supplement (ASEC) to the Current Population Survey (CPS) for 1981 and 2016.

- Excessive fees erode investment returns by up to 30 percent.
- When workers change jobs or make hardship withdrawals, 401(k) leakages drain retirement savings.
- Expecting individuals to manage living off a lump-sum payout for two or three decades is unrealistic. A predictable lifetime income stream is inherently more secure.

Given these many flaws, why has the 401(k) remained the primary retirement vehicle for so many Americans today? The answer is simple. Although the 401(k) is not the best option, in most cases it is the only option.

WHY 401(K)S FAIL SAVERS

The 401(k) fails the savers who need them most:

- 401(k)s do not accumulate enough savings. Across the United States, the median 401(k) account balance is $18,433. Less than 50 percent of 401(k) holders accumulate adequate savings for retirement.
- High administrative expenses erode savings over time (see figure.)
- 401(k)s are not close to universal; 53 percent of private sector workers lack access to any workplace retirement plan.
- 401(k)s and IRAs leave low- and middle-income families behind. Families in the top 20 percent of income distribution are ten times more likely to have a retirement savings account than those in the

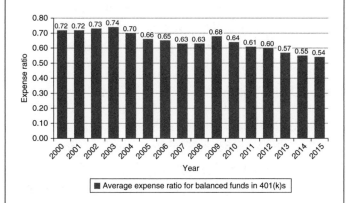

High administrative expenses erode savings over time.

Source: Investment Company Institute

(continued)

lowest 20 percent. These affluent savers benefit from tax incentives unavailable to most Americans. To heighten the inequity, affluent savers are more apt to work for larger employers with more generous employer plans, and they also can afford to take on greater investment risk, thereby earn higher returns on savings.

- Low-income families lack the wherewithal to save, even if they want to save. A recent Federal Reserve study showed that 47 percent of Americans would be unable to come up with $400 in an emergency.*

- 401(k)s and IRAs are structured in ways that constrain returns. Under Department of Labor regulations, fiduciary liability falls solely on providers, forcing them to offer simple investment options with full liquidity. As a result, these plans favor short-term investments that deliver much lower returns—sometimes by as much as half—when compared to defined-benefit portfolios.

- Even the top 10% won't have adequate retirement savings to replace anywhere close to their current standard of living.

- 401(k)s place the onus for saving, planning, and administration on the saver. Workers with 401(k)s must figure out how much they need to save, how that money should be invested, and—once they reach retirement—how to manage their assets so they do not outlive their savings. That is a mighty challenge for a savvy professional investor. It is an impossible burden for virtually everyone else.

- 401(k)s ignore human nature. Human beings are poorly wired to plan for the long term, especially if real wages are stagnant. When families must choose between fixing their car or replacing their bulky TV, or scrimping for a far off retirement, most will choose the more immediate need.
- Though some are changing, most 401(k)s are still voluntary, opt-in savings systems. Workers may also exit by liquidating savings at any time—in exchange for high fees and penalties.
- The government tax subsidies favor the wealthy.

---

* Board of Governors of the Federal Reserve System, "Report on the Economic Well-Being of U.S. Households in 2014," May 2015, https://www.federalreserve.gov/econresdata/2014-report-economic-well-being-us-households-201505.pdf.

RETIREMENT AND INEQUALITY

Retirement wealth is grossly unequal, leaving the bottom half with next to nothing. Of the 40 percent of households with savings from defined-contribution plans, most are in the top quartile of earners. Further, the median balance for white households ($58,000) is more than three times the median balance of black ($16,400) and Hispanic ($18,900) households.[10]

In fact, retirement wealth is distributed even less evenly than income (figure 2.2).

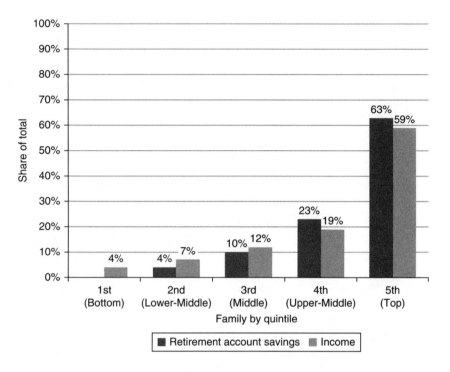

Figure 2.2 Share of total retirement account savings and total income for families in peak earning years (age 50–55) by income quintile, 2013.

An ongoing survey by the Employee Benefit Research Institute shows that a retirement plan is the biggest single factor in older workers' confidence in a secure retirement. Meanwhile, a Bankrate survey suggests that retirement anxiety is the new "class divide." When asked whether they were confident they were saving enough, people making more than $75,000 per year (the top 20 percent of earners) were three times more likely to answer in the affirmative than those earning less.[11]

The obstacles to adequate saving land unevenly by gender as well. Women tend to live longer than men, so they need more funds for retirement. Yet women generally have less retirement savings due to lower wages and careers interrupted by family duties. In addition, women are hit harder financially by divorce. According to Diane Oakley, executive director of the Retirement Security Institute, "Women are 80 percent more likely than men to be impoverished at age 65 and older, while women between the ages of 75 and 79 are three times more likely than men to be living in poverty."[12]

THE RETIREMENT CRISIS ILLUSTRATED THREE WAYS

Researchers measure the retirement readiness of U.S. workers in various ways. But regardless of the metric, the conclusion is invariably the same: without drastic, systemic reform, millions of today's middle-class workers will be tomorrow's poor or near-poor retirees. Let's look more closely at three yardsticks.

The first method tallies the total U.S. deficit in retirement income (also known as the retirement wealth gap) and puts a dollar figure on it akin to the national debt. To make this calculation, economists compare the wealth accumulated by working-age households to the wealth they will need to retire comfortably. The variable is a household's target income replacement rate in retirement, typically 65 to 75 percent.

(continued)

(*Continued*)

We don't need 100 percent of our preretirement income because certain expenses—such as work wardrobes, saving for retirement, and commuting costs—go away. The precise percentage of income replacement depends primarily on what you earned before you retired. Lower-income people need a higher replacement rate because necessities cost the same for everyone; higher-income workers need slightly less to maintain their standard of living.

After accounting for each household's wealth and income, including anticipated Social Security benefits, one can measure the gap between the projected actual replacement rate (what savers are on track to have) and the target replacement rate (what they will need to maintain their preretirement standard of living). Then the gaps for every U.S. household are added together.

According to some calculations, the nation's retirement wealth gap currently stands at $7.7 trillion, or 43 percent of U.S. gross domestic product (GDP The WEF, however, says the deficit could be as high as $27 trillion, or about 150 percent of GDP. Put another way, more than one and a half times our GDP would be required to get every household on track for a comfortable retirement.

A second way to measure retirement savings projects the replacement rate based on workers' current savings practices. This method highlights the limitations of Social Security in filling the retirement wealth gap. By itself, Social Security replaces only 41 percent of a median earner's income if the worker retired at age sixty-seven. Retiring earlier means Social Security replaces only 29 percent, illustrating the power of working longer if you can. These numbers have been in steady decline since the 1980s due to benefit cuts that continue to take effect.

In 2011, households with a defined-benefit pension were on track to achieve a 75 percent replacement rate—all to the good. But those with 401(k)s and other defined-contribution plans were on track for only a 62 percent replacement rate, beneath the floor for a secure retirement. Those with no plan at all were even worse off, projected at only a 57 percent replacement rate.[†] Without a defined-benefit plan, in other words, workers can expect their income in retirement to fall by roughly 40 percent, more than they can afford to lose and still maintain their standard of living.

Middle-income earners are hit hardest by this shortfall. A lifetime low-wage employee (someone earning around two-thirds the median, or $33,000 annually in 2016) can replace wages in retirement mostly with Social Security and a relatively small amount of income from retirement savings. By comparison, career-long earners of $100,000-plus will need to replace about 46 percent of their preretirement earnings with retirement wealth. Social Security will account for no more than 24 percent of their preretirement income. These Social Security replacement percentages are lower for people who retire prior to age sixty-seven, which most Americans, especially low-income people, are likely to do.

The third method compares real-life median retirement account balances to a target balance for an adequately fund retirement. For households to attain a 70 percent

(continued)

replacement rate, they need to save a sum equal to approximately eight to eleven times their annual salary by the time they retire.

Consider a head of household between fifty and sixty-five who earns the median annual income of $49,000 per year. This individual would need to save a minimum of $375,000 for a comfortable retirement at age sixty-five. But based on our analysis of the Survey of Consumer Finances, the median household in this group has saved only $12,000. When converted into an annuity (based on average life expectancy), $12,000 would pay just $50 a month.

Even excluding those without any plan at all, the median balance for all people nearing retirement is only $102,000. Aon Hewitt suggests that workers should have twice their annual salary saved by age thirty-five, seven and one-third times annual pay by age fifty-five, and eleven times annual pay by age sixty-five. Barely one in five workers meets those targets.[‡]

In conclusion, regardless of the yardstick, most workers fall into one of two categories. They either have an inadequate workplace retirement plan or they have no plan at all.

---

[*]Alicia H. Munnell, Anthony Webb, and Francesca Golub-Sass, "The National Retirement Risk Index: An Update," Center for Retirement Research at Boston College, October 2012, http://crr.bc.edu/briefs/the-national-retirement-risk-index-an-update/.

[†]Teresa Ghilarducci, Joelle Saad-Lesser, and Kate Bahn, "Are U.S. Workers Ready for Retirement? Trends in Plan Sponsorship, Participation, and Preparedness," *Pension Benefits Journal* (Winter 2015): 25–39.

[‡]Aon Hewitt, "The 2012 Real Deal: 2012 Retirement Income Adequacy at Large Companies: Highlights," Aon.com, 2012, http://www.aon.com/attachments/human-capital-consulting/The_2012_Real_Deal_Highlights.pdf.

A TICKING TIME BOMB

The preponderance of research confirms that most older workers have saved insufficiently for retirement. Barring reform, a shocking number are destined for poverty. The chief culprit is not the erosion of Social Security. It is the inadequate funding of workplace retirement accounts.

This trend is a political time bomb with potentially devastating effects on the federal deficit, state and local government budgets, and the macro economy. All will feel the detrimental consequences of our looming retirement crisis.

3

SIX KEY PROBLEMS

The Consequences of a Broken Retirement System

Primarily as a result of an overreliance on voluntary defined-contribution plans in the United States, six fundamental problems plague our nation's retirement system. Let's take a closer look at these challenges.

1 FEW WORKERS ACCUMULATE ENOUGH SAVINGS, EVEN IF OFFERED A WORKPLACE DEFINED-CONTRIBUTION PLAN

The shortfalls in retirement savings by U.S. workers are dramatic. In 2014, 52 percent of households included at least one person over fifty-five who had no retirement savings.[1] The Government Accountability Office (GAO) calculates the median balance held by retirees between fifty-five and sixty-four years of age at a mere $80,000.

Many retirees would like to move into an annuity, a financial instrument that exchanges their savings for a guaranteed yearly income for the rest of their lives. But if $80,000 were to be annuitized, the income would be $6,000 a year, or a paltry $453 a month.

2 PEOPLE WHO CONTRIBUTE TO DEFINED-CONTRIBUTION PLANS ARE LIKELY TO DIP INTO SAVINGS BEFORE RETIREMENT, INCURRING HIGH FEES AND TAXES IN THE PROCESS

The United States is one of the few nations that allow tax-preferred retirement savings like those in a 401(k) to be withdrawn before retirement. Most countries prohibit early withdrawals for any reason; a few make exceptions for a life-altering illness or other true emergencies. In the United States, you can withdraw your savings almost whenever you want, for any reason, but you must pay a hefty tax penalty.

On its face, a withdrawal option might seem logical. It is your money, after all. But when workers withdraw retirement savings prematurely, they suffer twice: first in fees and taxes, and second by losing the money's future compounding returns. One dollar taken out today costs more than three dollars in savings twenty years from now. The net result is weakened long-term financial security.

When individuals change jobs and move to an employer with an incompatible plan, they often make an early withdrawal. In fact, employers can and often do force departing employees with a balance of $5,000 or less to leave their 401k plans altogether in an effort to save administrative costs and reduce liability. With the added burden of paperwork to transfer and track their plan, many workers simply give up.

3 PARTICIPANTS IN DEFINED-CONTRIBUTION PLANS REALIZE SUBPAR RETURNS DUE TO HIGH FEES AND BEING FORCED TO PAY FOR LIQUIDITY THEY DO NOT NEED

Administrators of 401(k)s are required to offer predominantly short-term instruments with ample liquidity. That structural bias excludes 401(k)s and IRAs from longer-term, less liquid alternatives, leading to subpar returns in comparison to pension funds and endowments.

The constrained investment strategy, higher administrator fees, and lack of investment acumen of most 401(k) participants take their toll on returns. This can be seen in figure 3.1

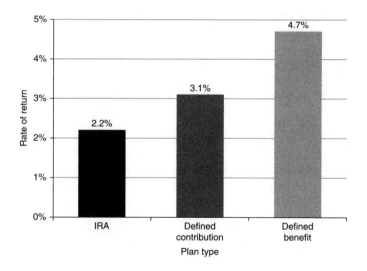

Figure 3.1 Geometric rates of return by plan type, 2000–2012.

Source: Center for Retirement Research at Boston College (2015) "Investment Returns: Defined Benefit vs. Defined Contribution Plans"

from a study by Boston College's Center for Retirement Research of investment results from 2000 to 2012. A Towers Watson study of investment returns from 1995 to 2008 shows similar results (figure 3.2). These two studies include both active and inactive (or "frozen") defined-benefit plans together. Because frozen plans move heavily to low-return fixed-income investments to lock in funding, the excess returns earned by active defined-benefit high-grade bond plans will tend to be understated.

A study by the National Institute on Retirement Security found that the all-in costs of providing the same level of benefits was 46 percent less in a defined-benefit plan than in a defined-contribution plan. More than half of this cost difference, 26 percent, was due to the ability of defined-benefit plans to earn superior investment returns.

Other studies show that defined-benefit plans achieved better returns over both longer and shorter periods. A National Association of State Retirement Administrators study showed the rate of return for public pension plans (median public pension fund's annualized rate of return) was 8.4 percent for the twenty-five-year period ending in June 2015 and 6.6 percent for the ten year period ending in June 2015. A more recent study through 2016 by Callan Associates also shows consistently higher returns in public pension plans (figure 3.3).[2] Public pension plans are the most relevant comparables for the proposed Guaranteed Retirement Account (GRA) pooled national fund because both are ongoing retirement trusts with similar time horizons, risk parameters, investment strategies, cash flows, and objectives.

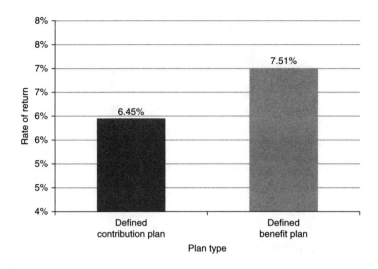

Figure 3.2 Rates of return by plan, 1995–2008.

Source: Willis Towers Watson. *DB Versus DC Plan Investment Returns: The 2008–2009 Update*. March, 2011.

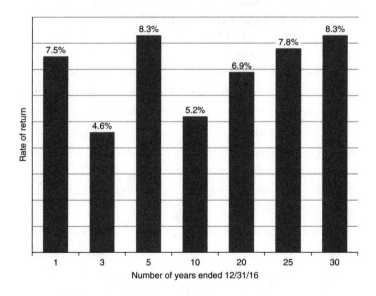

Figure 3.3 Median public pension annualized investment returns for periods ended 12/31/16.

Source: Callan Associates. NASRA Issue Brief: Public Pension Plan Return Assumptions, February 2017.

Historically, defined-contribution plans have delivered anemic returns compared to the returns of pension funds, which follow longer-term strategies. The drawbacks to this system are clear. A dollar earning a 3 percent nominal return over a forty-five-year career grows to less than four dollars. A dollar earning 6.5 percent over the same period grows to more than seventeen dollars—quite a difference! Simply put, limiting investment portfolios to high-liquidity investments hurts workers by shrinking their savings and making a secure retirement a long shot.

4 THE OVERALL ECONOMY MISSES THE FULL BENEFIT OF PEOPLE'S SAVINGS BECAUSE 401(K)S AND IRAS FAIL TO BUILD LONG-TERM CAPITAL FORMATION

Excessive short-term investing is not just bad for retirees; it hurts the entire nation. The accumulated retirement savings of the American people represents an enormous amount of capital that could be invested in anything from infrastructure and real estate to venture capital. These investments could be of tremendous benefit to our country, but our current retirement system makes them almost impossible.

For a view of the GRA's potential, we can look at other countries with national retirement plans similar to our proposal. Without exception, they report greater economic growth and stability. In Australia, national retirement savings actually exceed gross domestic product (GDP), creating a ballast that helped the country sidestep the global market calamity in 2008. As Susan Thorp, a professor at the University of Technology, Sydney, explains:

> If you have people making regular contributions from their wages, there's always this steady stream of inflows into the capital markets. . . . It's money that comes into the market to purchase securities regardless of conditions.[3]

There is no reason the United States cannot adopt a similar approach. In 2014, public sector pension funds represented 20 percent of U.S. venture capital.[4] GRAs can play a similarly vital role.

5 THE CURRENT SYSTEM FEATURES UPSIDE DOWN INCENTIVES: THE WEALTHY AND FINANCIALLY SOPHISTICATED RECEIVE TAX SUBSIDIES, AND LOW-INCOME AND MANY MIDDLE-CLASS WORKERS GET NONE

Each year, federal and state governments spend a total of $140 billion to subsidize affluent workers' 401(k) contributions.[5] But these tax breaks do little or nothing to help workers most at risk for an impoverished retirement. In fact, the sole federal tax incentives that directly benefit savers are steeply regressive. The top 20% most affluent Americans get more than 70 percent of the benefit from retirement tax deductions. The bottom 20% get almost nothing because they save very little and have low tax rates.

The sad irony is that affluent Americans often don't even rely on their 401(k) plans for retirement. They have access to more sophisticated investment vehicles; they can bear more investment risk to earn better long-term returns. For this group, 401(k)s are used less for retirement security than simply to cut their tax bills. And for the very wealthy—the 314 Americans who collectively have more than $80 billion in their 401(k)s—the accounts have nothing to do with retirement at all. They are instruments to accumulate even more wealth.[6]

WORKING LONGER IS NOT A SOLUTION FOR ALL AMERICANS

There are many benefits to working longer, but it is not the right strategy for everyone. No older person should be compelled to put off retirement to secure his or her financial future. According to a 2008 study by the Center for Retirement Research, disability rates among older Americans have risen for four consecutive decades.[*] Based on our analysis of the Health and Retirement Study panel, 33 percent of workers aged fifty-five to sixty-four have jobs that require heavy lifting, bending, stooping, or crouching all or most of the time. The incidence of these physical demands is higher among the poor, women, and minority workers.[†]

Even when people are physically able to work, older workers face an unfriendly labor market. On average, a jobless worker aged fifty-five or older spent thirty-six weeks looking for work in 2015, compared to twenty-six weeks for a jobless younger worker. Although "headline" unemployment (being jobless while actively job hunting) is typically lower for older individuals, many older workers give up looking for work despite wanting a job. They default to claiming Social Security early, which severely erodes their annual benefits for the rest of their lives. They are involuntarily retired but not counted as unemployed. In tracking an alternate unemployment rate that includes older workers who have given up looking—even in a "strong" labor market with only 5 percent official unemployment—we found about 12 percent of older Americans are unemployed or underemployed but want a job.[†]

[*] Alicia H. Munnell, Mauricio Soto, and Alex Golub-Sass, "Are Older Men Healthy Enough to Work?" Center for Retirement Research at Boston College, October 2008, no. 8-17, http://citeseerx.ist.psu.edu/viewdoc/download; jsessionid=6AF1E978B3986B4B74776E3E8D7DE4FD?doi=10.1.1.620.4393&rep=rep1&type=pdf.

[†] Teresa Ghilarducci, Bridget Fisher, Kyle Moore, and Anthony Webb, "Gender and Racial Disparities in Physical Job Demands of Older Workers," New School, Schwartz Center for Economic Policy Analysis, Policy Note, October 2016, http://www.economicpolicyresearch.org/images/docs/research/retirement_security/2016-4_Gender_Racial_Gaps_in_Older_Workers_Physical_Job_Demands.pdf.

[†] Author's calculation using the Current Population Survey for December 2016. Workers who fit these criteria are (1) counted in U-3 or "headline" unemployment; (2) counted in U-6 unemployment (marginally attached to the labor force or involuntary part-time); or (3) report wanting a job but are not counted in either U-3 or U-6 unemployment.

6 EVEN FOR FINANCIALLY SOPHISTICATED RETIREES, THE CURRENT SYSTEM OFFERS NO COST-EFFECTIVE MEANS TO CONVERT RETIREMENT SAVINGS INTO LIFELONG INCOME

Our national retirement system needs to keep pace with rising life expectancies and the corollary likelihood that people will be retired longer. In 1950, the average woman retired at age sixty-one and lived more than twenty years in retirement; the average man retired at sixty-four and lived another fourteen years. Today, women at age sixty-five can expect to live to be eighty-seven, and sixty-five-year-old men live to nearly eighty-four. Barring a jump in the average retirement age,[7] retirees will be living longer in retirement—and will need more funds to remain comfortable and secure. Yet most people cannot plan for an uncertain life span because they lack the expertise to properly invest and annuitize their savings. In fact, Nobel laureate William Sharpe calls 'decumulation,' or the use of savings in retirement, "the nastiest, hardest problem in finance." The number of potential outcomes are almost infinite, or as Sharpe describes it, a "multi-period problem with actuarial issues, in a multi-dimensional scenario matrix."[8]

Today's annuity plans are complex. They carry higher costs because of what economists call "adverse selection": when dealing with a riskier customer, you demand a higher price. Insurers anticipate that those purchasing annuities do so because they expect to live longer than average. Further, purchasers tend to be more affluent, with longer life expectancies.

To compensate for this longevity risk, insurers inflate the cost of annuities for everyone.

In the following chapters, we outline a solution that addresses all six of these problems and puts every American on the path to a sustainable retirement.

4

RESCUING RETIREMENT

A Four-Pronged Solution

The Guaranteed Retirement Account (GRA) was born out of an understanding that the United States faces a generational choice. It is not unlike the one we faced in 1929—six years before the enactment of Social Security—when the prospect of millions of elderly Americans living in poverty loomed, even before the Great Depression took its toll.

It was then that a young governor of New York, Franklin Delano Roosevelt, declared:

> No greater tragedy exists in modern civilization than the aged, worn-out worker who, after a life of ceaseless effort and useful productivity, must look forward for his declining years to a poorhouse. A modern social consciousness demands a more humane and efficient arrangement.[1]

Roosevelt was right for his time, and he is right for ours. As a society, it is our obligation to answer his call once again. Indeed, in a world in which the specter of widespread elder poverty has returned, we face a stark choice. Either we will rest with the status quo, consigning millions of our hardworking citizens to ending their lives in near or outright poverty, or we will seize the opportunity to solve the problem.

Here is the good news: we can solve this problem almost painlessly.

Our solution begins with individual savings, the foundation of the GRA. Why is our plan superior to the retirement instruments available today? Simply put, it makes contributions easier, cheaper and assured, it delivers a higher rate of return, and it ensures lifelong income when people retire.

In fact, the WEF lays out three principles for a successful retirement system design: safety net pension for all, access to well managed cost-effective plans, and incentives to increase contributions. Our plan has all of these elements.

A GRA has three basic components:

1. Every worker owns a portable retirement saving account. Workers maintain ownership of a government-guaranteed account over their career, automatically contributing at least 1.5 percent of each paycheck until they retire. A matching 1.5 percent—or more—is provided by employers. An additional $600 per year is contributed by the federal government.

2. Savings are pooled and invested to achieve higher returns. Workers select a pension manager, who invests pooled GRAs in a way that ensures they will earn higher returns with lower risk. These pension allocators may include state pension funds, traditional money managers, or a federal entity such as the Thrift Savings Plan. Workers can change managers annually at will, based on performance, fees, or other considerations.

WHO GETS A GRA, AND WHO CONTRIBUTES?

Under our plan, everyone with a Social Security number is identified. Any employee without access to an existing qualifying workplace retirement plan is automatically enrolled in a GRA. An individual with a 401(k) or any other plan—including part-time and self-employed workers—has the *option* to roll savings over to a higher-performing GRA. Workers choosing to keep their defined-benefit or 401(k) plan may opt to supplement it with voluntary contributions to a GRA. Voluntary contributions do not have to be annuitized and may be withdrawn as a lump sum on retirement. If implemented today, 85 million Americans who currently lack a retirement savings account would receive one under our plan.

3. Upon retirement, the account provides lifelong payments. Upon retirement, the bulk of the GRA is annuitized to guarantee consistent, lifelong income.

This new system represents a three-pronged solution to the retirement crisis:

1. The GRA ensures that all full-time workers can save enough to retire.
2. The GRA invests those savings in longer-term strategies with higher rates of return.
3. The GRA guarantees lifelong annuitized income, regardless of how long a retiree lives.

The remainder of this chapter explores each of these benefits in more detail.

WHAT LIFE LOOKS LIKE WITH GRAs

Zero Annual Cost

The cost of secure retirement to a median-salary worker who retires at age sixty-seven after tax credits.

6 to 7 Percent Annually (Nominal)

Expected annual return for GRA savings—versus 2 to 4 percent for typical 401(k)s and IRAs.

Universal Coverage

Every worker can own a fully portable GRA as a workplace supplement to Social Security, including 87 million Americans who currently lack access to retirement savings plans today. This especially helps older women and others intermittently in the workforce. It helps young people capture the advantage of saving early in their lives.

$127,000

Additional lifetime savings that a twenty-five-year-old contributing $600 a year could expect by age sixty-five with a GRA. In addition, this contribution would be wholly offset by a tax credit and thus is cost-free for almost all savers earning a median salary or less.

---

1 A GUARANTEED RETIREMENT ACCOUNT ENSURES THAT ALL WORKERS CAN SAVE ENOUGH TO RETIRE

What is surprising about the current retirement crisis is that, despite deep and widespread shortfalls, the additional yearly savings required for most Americans to secure their retirement is relatively small.

Consider the math. Today, Social Security represents the equivalent of saving 12.4 percent of annual income. With the addition of a higher-return GRA, we calculate that most full-time workers need to save an additional 3 percent per year over the course of their careers to maintain their standard of living in retirement. Although 3 percent may seem like a small number for such a large benefit, it is sufficient for most workers who work to age sixty-seven because GRA managers invest those savings more efficiently than does the current system, and much earlier in a person's career than the current system. Because of compound interest and returns, a person can save a much smaller share of their income if they start saving for retirement in their twenties than if they started in their thirties (see figure 4.1).

There is only one practical way to fill this 3 percent gap. The savings must be mandated for all workers, including those who work part-time or are self-employed.

Mandates are politically loaded these days. But given the calamity of our existing retirement system, nothing short of a mandate will do.

For most Americans, this "mandate to save is more like a gift.

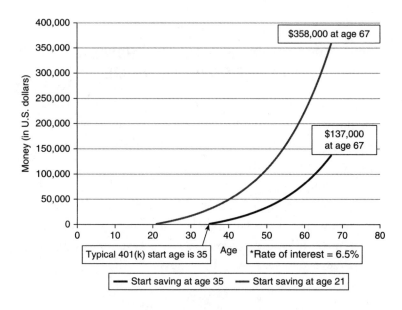

Figure 4.1 GRAs start with the first paycheck for larger balances.

Only a mandate can provide future generations of workers with adequate income for a secure retirement. For most Americans, this mandate is a gift—both costless and priceless. Through the combination of a tax credit and tax deductions, the GRA makes the worker's share of the contribution virtually free for most.

We would add that certain mandates—Social Security, for example—enjoy broad support from Americans today. Surmounting the political hurdle of a mandated 3 percent savings plan begins by splitting the GRA contribution evenly between employee and employer, similar to the arrangement for many 401(k) or 403(b) accounts today. Here is how this breakdown works.

IS 3 PERCENT ENOUGH?

Some retirement experts may be surprised by our assertion that a 3 percent total contribution is enough, but this is one of the beauties of the Guaranteed Retirement Account. By saving consistently from the very first paycheck, investing in higher-performing asset classes, and providing an efficient, federally administered annuity at retirement, our GRA plan requires a lower—and thereby more practical—savings rate.

Let's start with our definition of "enough." Studies by several experts, including economist Alicia Munnell, have estimated that individuals need 65 to 75 percent of preretirement income to maintain their lifestyle after they stop working. In retirement, people's expenditures come down, income tax rates are lower, and Medicare kicks in. As a result, retired workers need less income for a comfortable lifestyle. As a rule of thumb, a postretirement income of 70 percent is generally considered "enough."

For less affluent workers, much of that 70 percent comes from Social Security, which generally provides 25 to 50 percent of preretirement income, depending on the age of workers when they claim Social Security. Unfortunately, more than half of U.S. workers begin claiming Social Security before full retirement age (sixty-seven). These workers will need to either save more than 3 percent or work longer.

Like most of our discussion in this book, our focus here is on people earning less than $100,000 per year. Why? First, they are the ones most at risk in retirement. Second, they

(continued)

account for almost 92 percent of all U.S. workers.* Third, most individuals earning more than $100,000 per year can and do set aside personal savings beyond retirement plan minimums.

The gap between Social Security and 70 percent is what the GRA is projected to fill. A GRA by itself in conjunction with Social Security, with no other source of retirement income, is "enough" for workers earning $100,000 or less who retire at full retirement age.

Here is the math. Let's say Jane enters the workforce age twenty-two and works for forty-five years. About eighteen years in, assuming her entry pay is $30,000 and grows at 3 percent per year, she will be earning a median U.S. salary ($46,600 in 2015 dollars). Under a GRA plan, 3 percent of Jane's earnings would be contributed to her Guaranteed Retirement Account—1.5 percent from Jane and 1.5 percent from her employer. Our projected nominal net return for Jane, and for GRAs in general, is 6.5 percent per year over her career. (This is a conservative estimate, below historical pension returns or future returns projected by nearly every pension fund.) At age sixty-seven, when Jane retires, the balance of her GRA is converted into an annual annuity. Her annuity payments are based on her projected life span (to age eighty-seven) and that of her spouse, and assume an increase in the long-term government bond rate to 3.5 percent (compared to the 2.5 percent prevailing today).

Under these assumptions, Jane replaces 38 percent of her average preretirement income with her GRA annuity, and adds another 40 percent from Social Security.

Three Percent Provides an Adequate Savings Rate for Most People*

Lifetime Earnings	Annual Earnings in 2017	Replacement Rate from Social Security	Replacement Rate (average lifetime earnings) with Minimum GRA of 3%	Total Replacement Rate with Minimum GRA and Social Security
Maximum	$127,500	26%	38%	64%
High	$78,295	33%	38%	71%
Average	$48,937	40%	38%	78%
Low	$22,021	53%	38%	91%

* Assuming full retirement age.

(*Continued*)

> Her total replacement rate is 78 percent, comfortably above the 70 percent target. The table in this box shows approximate replacement rates for workers at different earnings levels.
>
> ---
>
> * Social Security Online, "Wage Statistics for 2015," Office of the Chief Actuary, June 15, 2017, https://www.ssa.gov/cgi-bin/netcomp.cgi?year=2015.

WHAT A 1.5 PERCENT CONTRIBUTION MEANS FOR EMPLOYEES

The employee's contribution of at least 1.5 percent is offset through two tax mechanisms, both of them deficit neutral and revenue neutral.

First, the GRA features a new refundable federal tax credit of up to $600 for all savers. For a person earning $40,000 a year, slightly above the U.S. median salary,[2] 1.5 percent of his or her annual income amounts to $600.[3] This means that the median-salaried worker's net cost for retirement security—via annual contributions of $1,200, including the employer's share—is zero.

On top of the $600 credit, the plan allows any workers whose 1.5 percent contribution exceeds $600 to deduct the difference from their taxes. For example, if a worker is earning $80,000 per year and makes a mandated contribution of $1,200, $600 is returned as a tax credit and the remaining $600 is tax-deductible. The employee effectively saves and invests $1,200 while paying only about $396, a net of tax savings-to-cost ratio of 3 to 1. When we include the employer's matching $1,200, total savings are $2,400, or 6.1 times the worker's actual cost of $396.

Our GRA model specifically helps low-wage, hourly workers, who benefit from a minimum employer contribution of fifteen cents per hour. In addition, our plan complements the IRS Saver's Credit by providing additional retirement security for households with a modest income.[4]

HOW ARE GRA TAX BENEFITS DEFICIT NEUTRAL?

The federal government already spends about $120 billion annually on tax deductions for defined-contribution plans, and states spend another $20 billion. These deductions disproportionately benefit the wealthiest Americans. GRAs redistribute this spending more evenly, across all workers, offering meaningful retirement savings support to those who need it most.

An analysis by the Tax Policy Center at The Urban Institute shows that the GRA plan means a stunning 61 million households without a retirement plan, will now get one. The GRA will also significantly help—with lower costs, better investments, consistent contributions and life-long income—many of the 66 million households who currently have a retirement plan, however ineffectual. Based on the TPC's work on key elements of the GRA plan and our analysis of other features, we believe that the GRA plan will be essentially revenue neutral when mature.

(continued)

(*Continued*)

Under the current system, over 60 million workers receive annually an average of $4,500 from their employers and $5,700 from the federal government in the form of tax breaks. But averages hide a crucial fact: the incentive is highly skewed—most of the subsidies go to people who already have the means to comfortably save for retirement. Taxpayers earning above $500,000 per year—about 1 percent of taxpayers—now get 43 percent of the government contributions to retirement accounts. Under our plan the three-quarters of taxpayers earning less than $100,000 per year will get about half of the benefits, making the whole system fairer and better aligning the government incentives. Under our plan, the 61 million households who have no retirement plan—and thus get no help from either the government or employers—will have an account and will get contributions from both.

To help retain deficit neutrality, our plan includes a provision whereby the income on super-sized IRAs (more than $5 million) would no longer be tax deferred. This would affect only about nine thousand people. (An amazing fact: there are 314 people who have IRAs worth $25 million or more.) In addition, the GRA will reduce the cost of other government support programs such as the Supplemental Security Income program because there will be fewer retirees in poverty. Furthermore, when the GRA starts to pay annuities to retiring participants, these payments will generate additional government tax receipts on the supplemental income. Finally, the health and emotional benefits from vast numbers of vulnerable Americans having a reasonably secure retirement are incalculable from a societal perspective, and there is substantial evidence that there will be large tangible cost savings in healthcare, homelessness, crime and drug addiction.

To go one step further, tackling the retirement crisis head-on will save taxpayers money in the long run. By reducing the number of seniors burdening Medicaid, public housing, and the Supplemental Nutrition Assistance Program (SNAP), for example, the GRA system significantly reduces future federal spending.

The GRA system is structured to help savers across the income spectrum, even affluent ones. For high-income workers, obligatory GRA contributions are capped at $3,750, or 1.5 percent of an annual salary cap of $250,000 of income. Like everyone else, these high-paid workers get the $600 GRA tax credit and can deduct the remainder—in this case, $3,050, for nearly a 2.5:1 ratio of savings to cost. With the employer's matching $3,750, they receive almost five dollars in retirement savings contributions for every dollar of net cost.

All workers are free to make additional GRA contributions beyond the required minimum, with the same annual limits that govern today's 401(k)s: $18,000 for individuals under age fifty and $24,000 for those fifty or over. Individuals may find it convenient and lucrative to save as much as possible in their professionally managed, low-fee, low-risk

GRA, which protects their principal (see appendix A). Extra contributions benefit from the same government guarantee, with returns accruing on a tax-deferred basis and that may be withdrawn as a lump sum upon retirement.

The GRA model also benefits public employees across the United States. Although many states and localities have sound pension programs, some are leaning toward freezing their defined-benefit plans and moving people to defined-contribution plans. Some public sector pensions are dangerously underfunded and at risk of failing. Existing public employee supplemental plans, such as the 457 plans, have been woeful performers with egregious expense levels. Contrary to policy-maker assumptions, these public sector workers can be at risk of an insecure retirement. They may need GRAs to replace or supplement their defined-benefit plans.

For all salaried savers, employee contributions to a GRA would be made as automatic payroll deductions by the employer similar to the way payroll taxes are currently deducted. Enforcement and penalties would be similar. Even for someone who had multiple employers or intermittent work, it should be simple: 3 percent of any wage or salary payment (1.5 percent from the employee and 1.5 percent from the employer) would be deducted from the payment and contributed to the GRA. Everyone with a Social Security number is automatically identified and enrolled.

For the self-employed, partnerships, or Subchapter S corporations, individuals are responsible for both the employer and employee shares of the mandatory GRA contribution, just as they are with Social Security.

WHAT THE 1.5 PERCENT CONTRIBUTION MEANS FOR EMPLOYERS

At the root of the gaps in today's voluntary pension system is competition. Employers hesitate to offer retirement plans for fear they will be placed at a disadvantage. Many also worry about the Employment Retirement Income Security Act (ERISA) of 1974, the federal law that sets pension plan standards, with its complex rules and potential liability. As a result, employers—and especially small business owners—are inhibited from providing for their employees.

Employer contributions are crucial to guarantee a secure retirement. The GRA model maintains a level playing field by mandating that all employers contribute at least 1.5 percent of their workers' salaries into one of three vehicles: a traditional pension plan, a defined-contribution plan, or a GRA. Because a GRA will cost the least to administer, we expect many businesses to choose this option.

All firms currently without a defined-benefit plan or a defined-contribution plan will automatically be enrolled in a GRA plan after five years. Employers with existing retirement plans also may offer a GRA option. To ease their transition to GRAs, businesses with fewer than five employees will have employer contributions waived for their first five years of participation.

Employer contributions are affordable:

- Employers deduct their share of GRA contributions, as they do with pension and other retirement plan contributions today.

- The cost of employer contributions is substantially offset by relief from the burdensome administration of existing plans. Many employers will save by eliminating the administrative and contribution costs associated with 401(k)s. (Note: Employers converting their 401(k) plans to GRAs are prohibited from reducing their current contribution levels for two years.)
- For employers establishing employee retirement plans for the first time, the modest added cost of a GRA plan can be covered by a slight increase in the prices they charge (usually less than 2 percent) or by the increase in productivity that may come with more satisfied and secure employees. With inflation widely regarded as too low, and productivity needing a boost, these effects should be manageable. Alternatively, implementation of the plan could cause a temporary, but small, dip in profitability. However, corporate profits are near an all-time high as a percentage of GDP, so this too should be manageable.
- Employers are required to contribute on only the first $250,000 of an employee's wages, although they would be free to pay more.
- Finally, the GRA model forestalls the need for a sharp increase in taxes to handle the retirement crisis, which will otherwise overwhelm government finances. For businesses, it is a smart tradeoff.

As employers compete for employees, retirement plans have emerged as an important recruiting tool in certain markets, leading to regional variations. In some areas, the norm is for employers to provide retirement plans; in others, the norm is to be pension-free. A Pew Charitable Trust study found that 71 percent of employees in Grand Rapids, Michigan, have access to a workplace retirement plan. But in heavily populated Florida and Texas in the South, fewer than 35 percent of employees can save for retirement at work.

Regardless of location, a 401(k)s high per-employee costs, on top of onerous ERISA requirements, are a deterrent for small businesses. In 2016, less than 20 percent of companies with fewer than twenty-four employees sponsored any kind of retirement plan. Small businesses are often like families, and owners know and care about their employees. A 2016 Pew survey found that small firms would welcome an easy solution to their employees' retirement problems.[5] The simply administered, low-overhead GRA model would enable many small employers to do what they have wanted to do all along—take care of their workers in retirement.

GRAs liberate employers from determining investment options, negotiating fees, distributing accumulations, archiving records, or assessing performance. Many ERISA regulations become moot. Today, when small employers sponsor a 401(k)-type plan, they are scrutinized by the U.S. Department of Labor. With GRAs, the employer would be responsible only for timely payroll deductions of GRA contributions (both its share and the employee's), alongside FICA and unemployment insurance. All contributions are funneled to a federal clearinghouse. Federal infrastructure is already in place that could process the contributions and, ultimately, deliver monthly GRA annuity checks.

LET'S PAUSE TO ANSWER A QUICK QUESTION: DOES THE GRA PROVIDE SUFFICIENT INCENTIVES TO SAVERS?

We believe the answer is an emphatic "yes," especially when compared to today's patchwork of retirement savings plans. Under the current retirement system, the government disproportionately subsidizes retirement savings for a small number of relatively affluent Americans. With GRAs, all savers will gain the opportunity to deduct their 1.5 percent contributions—and for many, their cost will be entirely offset by the $600 tax credit.

To ensure a secure and comfortable retirement, some workers may choose to contribute more than their mandated minimum of 1.5 percent. Many employers will be incentivized to do the same, just as many now enhance their 401(k) plans to attract and retain high-level employees. In addition, evidence from similar retirement systems around the globe (from Australia, in particular) suggests that systems do not need to match or tax-incentivize every dollar to get people to save. Many employees will want to contribute more than 3 percent to a safe, convenient, and high-performing option at their fingertips.

Indeed, after individuals have established a rainy day fund for emergency withdrawals (usually in a standard savings account), a GRA would be one of the more compelling vehicles for saving additional income toward retirement. It offers a higher return than a savings account and carries lower risk than a stock index fund. In addition, its return compounds on a tax-deferred basis.

2 GRAs INVEST IN LOWER-RISK, LONGER-TERM STRATEGIES THAT GENERATE A HIGHER RATE OF RETURN

Once workers accumulate savings, their money can—and must—work harder for them. IRAs and 401(k)s simply do not perform well enough. Fees are too high, and typical portfolios are poorly diversified.

People's money can—and must—work harder for them.

In short, too many individuals earn subpar returns on their retirement savings. The GRA model addresses this problem by shifting to a more institutional strategy. It also provides an additional layer of protection—the pension manager—between the saver and Wall Street. Pension managers will have a fiduciary duty solely to the GRA holders.

Without compromising individuals' direct ownership of their GRA savings, our plan invests that money as a unit of a broader strategic investment pool of GRAs from across the country. When people combine their funds, they increase their investing power. They can build more diversified portfolios and gain access to institutional-quality investment products. The result: a significantly higher return than most individuals can achieve on their own.

Managing pooled GRAs benefits savers in three ways. First, pooled investments leverage economies of scale to secure lower fees. As a recent study found, "The annual savings from transitioning from retail to institutional shares may be as high as 65 basis points (or 0.65 percent) per year."[6] In contrast to 401(k)s, where the biggest discounts are reserved for the largest employers, GRAs will offer lower fees across the board.[7] The pension managers' boards of trustees, whose roles are strictly fiduciary, contract with investment managers and account administrators for the best possible terms and performance.[8]

Second, a larger pool of capital gains entrée to top-tier portfolio managers, who compete to generate the best return. Historically, retirement plan participants with access to professional asset managers earn over 3 percent more annually than those who do not have such access.[9]

Third, and perhaps most important, these investment strategists adopt long-term investment horizons to generate the best results. The GRA pool taps opportunities typically reserved for institutional investors—less liquid, higher-return asset classes. These include high-yielding and risk-reducing alternatives such as real estate, private equity, venture capital, and hedge funds. Beyond enhancing returns, these investment products can provide downside protection. Their risk diversification protects families from precarious drops in liquid markets such as those we witnessed from 2007 to 2010, when the median household lost more than half of its retirement account savings. Many people do not understand that including these "alternative" asset classes in a portfolio actually reduces the overall risk of the portfolio because the performance of these assets is not highly correlated with core public market investments. The higher return and diversification benefits from these alternative assets more than offsets the fact that such assets can individually carry a higher risk in isolation (figure 4.2).

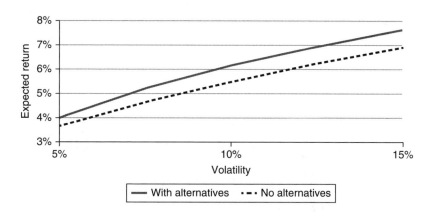

Figure 4.2 Illiquid or alternative assets reduce risk for a given level of return.

When institutions using this longer-term investment strategy are surveyed, superior results are clear (figure 4.3):

- Over a twenty-five-year investment period, professionally run public pension funds delivered an 8.5 percent median rate of return.[10]
- A Vanguard survey of university endowments with long-term investment horizons found similar success: an average return of 8.4 percent over twenty-five years.

A well-designed retirement savings vehicle allows savers to take prudent risks—particularly in long-term investments—and thereby earn higher returns. The GRA plan facilitates risk-sharing and exposure over long-term cycles in pooled plans managed by professionals.

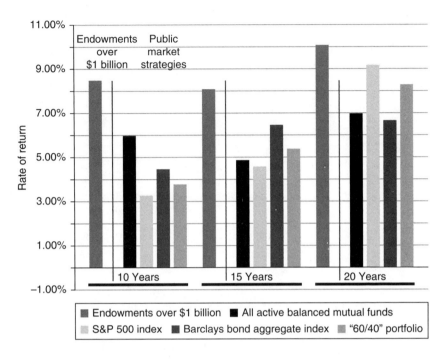

Figure 4.3 Larger endowments, able to adopt more sophisticated investment strategies, have outperformed public market strategies over time.

Source: Vanguard Research (2014) "Assessing Endowment Performance: The Enduring Role of Low Cost Investing," *Source*: *The Balance*, Historic Returns; and author's analysis

Because GRA savers will make steady, annual contributions, their accounts will benefit from a long-term, dollar-cost-averaging investment strategy. When they put the same amount of capital to work each year, investors automatically buy more in weak markets (when prices are lower) and less in peak markets (when prices are high). In voluntary plans, people's natural instinct is just the opposite. They plough into overpriced stocks when the market is surging to new highs,

THE GRA IS A HYBRID DEFINED-BENEFIT PLAN

The GRA is a hybrid defined-benefit plan, with flexible contributions, full portability, and a guaranteed monthly payout for the rest of the worker's life. Defined-benefit plans earn higher returns than defined-contribution plans.

Because of fees, leakages, and other systemic flaws in the 401(k) system, savings are severely eroded. Defined-contribution returns generally do not match the returns provided by defined-benefit plans. Defined-benefit pensions—the most popular form of workplace retirement plan before the 401(k) system was introduced—earned a 4.7 percent return between 2000 and 2012. Defined-contribution plans, including 401(k)s, earned a 3.1 percent return over the same period. IRAs earned a slim 2.2 percent return.[*]

---

[*] Alicia Munnell, Jean-Pierre Aubry, and Caroline C. Crawford, "Investment Returns: Defined Benefit vs. Defined Contribution Plans," Center for Retirement Research at Boston College, December 2015, no. 15-21, http://crr.bc.edu/wp-content/uploads/2015/12/IB_15-21.pdf.

then panic and retreat to money market funds as the market plummets—when equity values can be greatest. The GRA mechanism both rationalizes the investment process and dampens volatility over time.

In nearly every asset class, investors earn higher returns from illiquid assets versus liquid assets with comparable risk. People pay a premium for flexibility (figures 4.4 and 4.5).

The problem is that many investors are paying for far more liquidity than they actually need, especially in their 401(k)s.

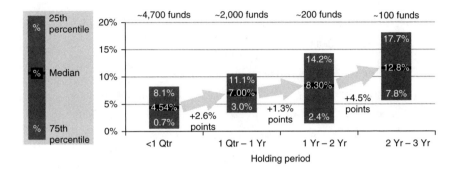

Figure 4.4 Less liquid hedge funds offer a return advantage.

Sources: "Expected Returns," by Amtti Illmanen, 2011. Scatterplotting average asset returns 1990–2009 on (subjective) illiquidity estimates. (Bloomberg, MSCI Barra, Ken French's website, Citigroup, Barclays Capital, JP Morgan, Bank of America Merrill Lynch, S&P GSCI, MIT-CRE, FTSE, Global Property Research, UBS, NCREIF, Hedge Fund Research, Cambridge Associates).

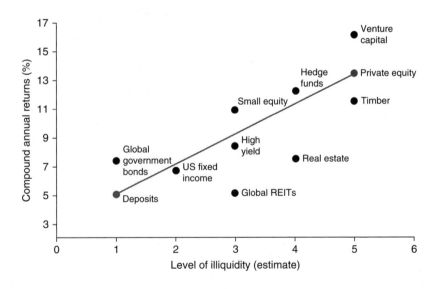

Figure 4.5 Investment returns generally increase with degree of illiquidity.

Source: National Association of State Retirement Administrators (2017), "Issue Brief: Public Pension Plan Investment Return Assumptions."

Because these accounts theoretically can be redeemed in full at any time, they are required to have daily liquidity, a constraint that saps their performance. Perhaps more than any other one factor, the anemic returns of 401(k)s have sabotaged retirement security and led to the current crisis.

What About Future Returns?

It is impossible, of course, to forecast with certainty what the pooled assets in a GRA plan will earn. But decades of past performance suggest that pooled long-term funds significantly outperform 401(k)s and other defined-contribution plans. After fees, these plans tend to earn 2 to 4 percent annually—not enough to grow a saver's nest egg to where it needs to be. Most of us would benefit from a longer-term approach. We are confident that GRAs can target an annual nominal rate of return of 6 to 7 percent.

A substantial majority of pension plans assume future returns of between 7 and 8 percent per year.

Figure 4.6 shows the distribution of investment return assumptions from NASRA's Public Fund Survey, 2017. For comparison, projected forward returns of liquid assets are shown in figure 4.7.

This disparity has dramatic implications. For a twenty-five-year-old worker saving $1,200 per year, a 3 percent return will build to $101,000 in savings at age sixty-five; raise the return to 6.5 percent, and that nest egg grows to $256,000 (figure 4.8). When compounded over long periods, even a modestly higher return has a huge impact.

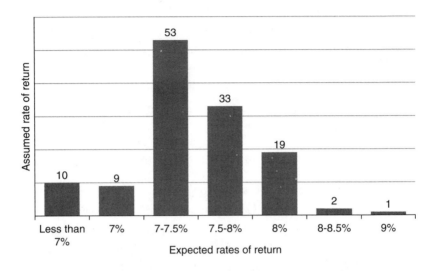

Figure 4.6 Expected five-year returns across traditional asset classes illustrate how a typical stock-and-bond strategy underperforms public pension funds.

Source: Goldman Sachs (2016) "2015 Outlook: The Last Innings." Investment Management Divison

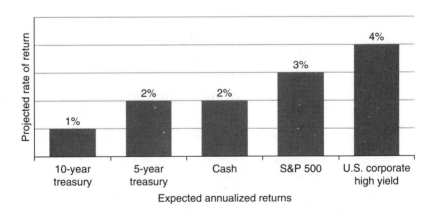

Figure 4.7 Differences in rate of return can create significantly different savings over time.

Source: Based on author's calculations

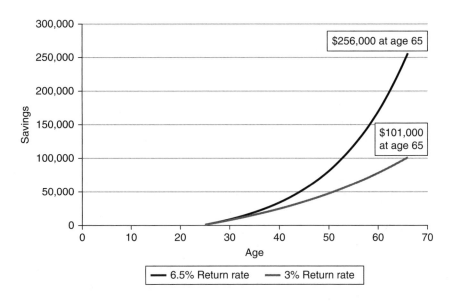

Figure 4.8 Modest changes in return rate yield huge impacts over long periods of time.

When workers start saving for retirement early, it makes a big difference. Many young people wait to begin saving and fall behind.

The GRA system's superior returns will go a long way toward closing the retirement wealth gap, and will do so free of charge. Indeed, the added "patient" capital available to be invested in growth initiatives should increase productivity, enhance U.S. competitiveness, and create jobs. For workers earning the median income or below, our plan takes no extra money from their paychecks. GRAs don't substantially increase employers' costs. Nor do they add to the federal deficit.

To protect all savers, GRAs are grounded in a governance structure that is professional, accountable, transparent, and dedicated to open public communication. Oversight of each GRA pension manager is properly the responsibility of a professional board of trustees. These pension managers also will be required to meet standards consistent with those of the Qualified Professional Asset Manager (QPAM) and state pension systems. They will have a fiduciary duty solely to GRA holders and will provide a layer of protection and oversight between the holders and Wall Street.

To allay savers' anxiety, the GRA plan takes an extra step, which will make it one of the safest savings options available. Under our GRA model, the federal government guarantees each saver's principal at the time of retirement. From that point forward, every individual will get back—as a guaranteed minimum—at least as much as he or she has put into the account.

This guarantee achieves two things. First, it smooths the threat of market volatility for those who retire in a down market. Second, it engenders confidence in the system. By granting participants peace of mind, the guarantee fortifies people's willingness to contribute more into the system.

The principal protection guarantee does not safeguard the GRA from losses in any single year, or even in multiple years. It simply means that workers' contributions over their careers are protected. At minimum, their GRA accounts will equal their total savings.

The guarantee functions as a onetime test at the point of retirement, when the GRA is annuitized. It is not discretionary or optional; it is baked into the annuity's calculation. Only payments up to the 401(k) limits ($18,000 or $24,000 per year, depending on age), along with employer matching contributions, including funds deposited when employees roll 401(k) savings into their GRAs, are covered by the guarantee.

A full protection of principal might sound like a large and controversial commitment by the federal government. In reality, it is a promise that is essentially costless. Based on longstanding historical trends, GRAs are highly likely to perform better than 0 percent over the long term. In our analysis of every rolling forty-year period since 1945, not one would have triggered the guarantee—even for seniors who retired amid the global financial crisis of 2007–2010. (For more details on why the principal protection guarantee is essentially costless, see appendix A.)

All the same, the government might charge a small insurance premium to cover this unlikely contingency. A fee of 0.015 percent of pay—less than $10 a year for a worker making $65,000—would build a reserve fund to cover potential costs in even the most extreme scenarios. We propose that the nonpartisan Congressional Budget Office score the cost of the guarantee and, using that cost, set premiums so there would be no cost to the government. As discussed in more detail in appendix A, we expect those premiums to start very low and to decline over time to nearly zero.

3 THE GUARANTEED RETIREMENT ACCOUNT ASSURES LIFELONG ANNUITIZED BENEFITS, NO MATTER HOW LONG A RETIREE LIVES

A well-designed retirement plan is built for lifetime income. Unfortunately, even among those who manage to save and invest their savings effectively, most lack the expertise to manage their savings to generate the right amount of income when they retire. Under the 401(k) model, the individual retiree shoulders the entire burden of postretirement asset management:

- Retirees must determine how best to invest or annuitize their retirement savings, a complex decision beyond most people's expertise.
- Retirees must bear the risk that the insurance company paying the annuity may become insolvent decades down the road.
- Retirees must pay for administrative costs and the insurance company's profit, which lowers the payments.

GRAs will guarantee retired individuals a set monthly minimum, based on their savings, for as long as they or their spouses live. (Retirees also can include children with disabilities and other long-term dependents, although this reduces the monthly annuity payment.) And GRAs are far more efficient, removing the guesswork and virtually all fees and expenses that gouge away at a nest egg.

For GRA beneficiaries, the transition to retirement will more or less replicate the experience of a traditional, defined-benefit pension plan.

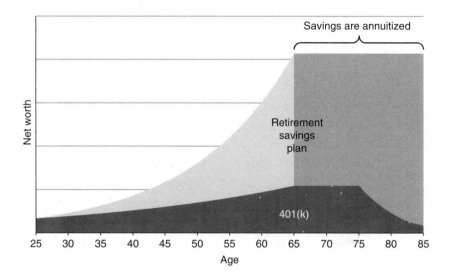

Figure 4.9 How annuitization meets the challenge of rising life expectancies.

The GRA restores what workers liked best about the defined-benefit system: certainty and peace of mind in retirement. It also relieves the individual of the burden of postretirement planning, a benefit in itself.

Annuitization meets the challenge posed by rising life expectancies. On average, today's retirees must stretch their savings fifteen to twenty years. With a defined contribution plan, if their savings run out, they are on their own (figure 4.9).

Guaranteed income, no matter how long a retiree or his or her spouse lives.

Individuals decide when to annuitize their GRAs, which can be any time after they become eligible for Social Security. Their options range from the point of disability to sixty-two (Social Security's early retirement age) to any age up to seventy when Social Security benefits max out. Within the sixty-two to seventy age bracket, savers also may choose to annuitize their GRA before collecting Social Security, deferring Social Security payments in exchange for a higher benefit.

Some retirees need liquid money in their transition from work to retirement, perhaps to adjust their lifestyle or to move. Under the GRA model, beginning at age sixty-two, individuals can withdraw up to 25 percent of their accumulated mandatory GRA payments as a lump sum. The sole restriction is that their remaining GRA balance, when annuitized and combined with Social Security, must keep them above the poverty line. (In 2017, for a median-income worker, this amounted to about $900 a month.) With respect to contributions over the mandatory minimum and the accumulated earnings on those amounts, annuitization is voluntary. In other words, the retiree decides how much to annuitize and how much to take as a lump sum. All withdrawals, including monthly annuity income payments, are subject to income taxes under prevailing tax law.

The GRA's individually owned annuities will be calculated by the existing U.S. Treasury Department's Federal Insurance Office (based on projected longevity at the time) and purchased from the U.S. government. The risk of increasing longevity would be the government's responsibility. Accordingly, the government would use the most current actuarial projections to take this risk into account. The Social Security Administration is the annuity payer, meaning payments are made through its existing infrastructure. No added bureaucracy or new government agency is required. In fact, with more assets under administration, Social Security administrative costs per person should decrease.

FAST FACTS ABOUT THE GRA ANNUITY

Annuitization doesn't stop you from returning to work. If a retiree goes back to work, he or she starts a new GRA while continuing to receive the original GRA's annuity payments. Upon retiring a second time, the individual receives the annuitized value of the second GRA added to the original annuity.

Annuities take into account the beneficiary's age and family structure at the date of retirement. For example, if a single, older retiree and a younger couple had the same GRA balance, the single older person would receive larger monthly payments. All workers receive the full value of their GRAs based on actuarial data.

Annuity payments are calculated to minimize the risk of unusually low annuity rates at the time of retirement. When calculating federal annuity payments, the plan uses the trailing five-year-average, long-term Treasury bond rate as the discount rate. This smooths out any volatility that new retirees might otherwise encounter.

Voluntary contributions in excess of the GRA minimums and the returns on them can be taken out as a lump sum if the retiree chooses to do so.

(*continued*)

(Continued)

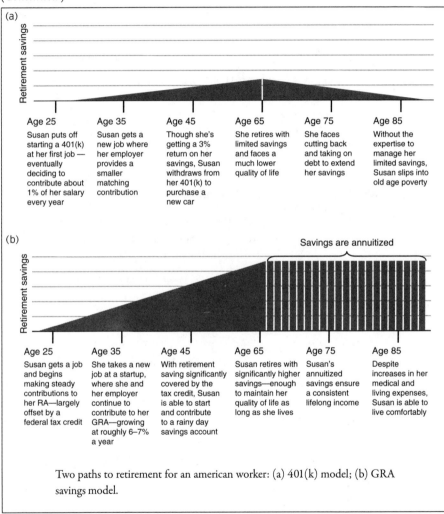

Two paths to retirement for an american worker: (a) 401(k) model; (b) GRA savings model.

ANNUITIES ENHANCE RETIREE SATISFACTION

Without a lifelong pension to supplement Social Security, older Americans suffer increased anxiety. Even those with healthy defined-contribution plans harbor a fear of outliving their retirement savings. Research shows that older people experience a greater sense of well-being with steady and assured income, as opposed to lumps of cash with variable returns.[*]

Let's compare two sixty-five-year-old retirees. One has a $250,000 IRA that must be managed to last the rest of his life. The other has a pension valued at $250,000 that pays him $1,500 per month in perpetuity, no matter how long he lives. Who is happier? Hands down, says the research, it is the retiree with the lifelong guaranteed annuity. Economists Steve Nyce and Billie Jean Quade find "that when comparing retirees with similar levels of health and wealth, those with annuitized incomes are the happiest."[†]

Even among retirees with little wealth and those in poor health, annuities help them feel better about their lives. The most satisfied retirees own traditional pension annuities and can flexibly choose when to retire. Annuities provide more satisfaction than equivalently valued lump sums.[‡] And while income and wealth are factors in overall well-being, a guaranteed income for life has a greater positive effect.[**]

---

[*] Teresa Ghilarducci, Bridget Fisher, and Zachary Knauss, "Now Is the Time to Add Retirement Accounts to Social Security: The Guaranteed Retirement Account Proposal," Schwartz Center for Economic Policy Analysis and Department of Economics, The New School for Social Research, Policy Note Series, 2015, www.economicpolicyresearch.org/images/docs/retirement_security . . . /GRA_3.0.pdf

[†] Steve Nyce and Billie Jean Quade. "Annuities and Retirement Happiness," Willis Towers Watson, 2012, https://www.towerswatson.com/en/insights/newsletters/americas/insider/2012/annuities-and-retirement-happiness.

[‡] Constantijn Panis, "Annuities and Retirement Satisfaction," Labor and Population Program, Working Paper 03-17, RAND, April 2003, https://www.rand.org/content/dam/rand/pubs/drafts/2008/DRU3021.pdf.

[**] Keith Bender and Natalia Jivan, "What Makes Retirees Happy?" An Issue in Brief no. 28, Center for Retirement Research at Boston College, February 2005, http://crr.bc.edu/wp-content/uploads/2005/02/ib_28.pdf .

4 GUARANTEED RETIREMENT ACCOUNTS REWARD OLDER AMERICANS FOR WORKING LONGER, IF THEY ARE WILLING AND ABLE

For many, working longer has financial, emotional, and health benefits. No one should be forced to leave the workforce before he or she is ready. Guaranteed Retirement Accounts facilitate this option for more people.

GRAs reward older workers who choose to stay in the workforce and gain more time to save for retirement. In general, this group becomes able to make larger contributions, and with fewer years in retirement, their savings do not need to stretch as far.

No one should be forced to leave the workforce before he or she is ready.

Under the GRA model, retiring later remains entirely optional. We are not proposing to increase the age to receive Social Security benefits. We also recognize that working longer may not be a viable option for everyone, including people with health issues and those working dangerous or physically demanding jobs.

The added GRA benefit from working longer is substantial. Working until age seventy rather than retiring at age sixty-two generates a much higher retirement income for four reasons:

1. A 35 percent bump in Social Security benefits.
2. Eight additional years of accumulated investment returns on the individual's GRA balance before annuitization.
3. Eight additional years of GRA contributions and their compounded returns.

4. Substantially higher annuity payments, from both compounding a larger GRA balance and reduced longevity upon annuitization (because the individual is older at retirement). In total, annual postretirement income— combining the added benefits from both Social Security and a GRA—grows by almost 70 percent!

Here is the simplified math: A man who has earned the median income ($47,000) during his career who waits to retire at age seventy would have a balance in his GRA of $424,000, compared to $248,000 for a comparable man who retired at sixty-two (assuming a 6.5 percent annual investment return). This represents a 66 percent increase. The seventy-year-old would have a remaining life expectancy of fourteen years versus twenty years for the sixty-two-year-old. As a result, the seventy-year-old would have an annuity from his GRA more than 2.1 times that of the sixty-two-year-old. Because delaying Social Security claiming to age seventy also increases Social Security benefits by 35 percent, the person claiming at seventy would receive a combined GRA annuity plus Social Security payment almost 70 percent higher in aggregate than that of the sixty-two-year-old! Even if someone cannot work all the way to seventy, each additional year worked is significantly beneficial. This clearly illustrates the benefits of not retiring early.

On the employer side, our model makes Medicare the primary health coverage for all people over sixty-five, even if they keep working. Employers covering health insurance get a substantial break for every employee past Medicare age. Instead of paying out $25,000 for an older worker's health insurance, the employer pays $2,000 to $5,000 for a Medicare supplement—a big incentive to keep older employees on the payroll longer. This simple change comes with little cost to the government. After all, Medicare would be paying anyway if the worker had retired.

HOW WILL THE PLAN BE IMPLEMENTED?

Implementing any large-scale plan requires a transition. Given the scope of the changes required and the numbers of people involved, we think it would be prudent to chart a five-year transition period for GRAs. A possible schedule might look like this.

Year One: A national marketplace of approved pension managers is formed, with each manager going through an appropriate registration and approval process. The Federal Thrift Savings plan or state pension funds are designated as the initial default managers. The Treasury Department in concert with the Social Security Administration and the pension managers begin to develop the systems needed to handle GRAs.

Year Two: Every worker is informed of the new plan. The Social Security Administration and the U.S. Treasury set up accounts. Workers with existing retirement account balances can exercise their option to roll their balances into a GRA.

Year Three: Workers and employers in any business with more than five employees, along with the self-employed, begin contributing to a GRA plan. Similar to workers who continue to contribute to a 401(k) or IRA, they receive a refundable tax credit of up to $600. The tax deductibility of new contributions to 401(k)s and IRAs is eliminated.

Year Four: GRA annuity payments commence.

Year Five: Small businesses with fewer than five employees also establish GRAs.

5

CASE STUDIES

Similar Plans in Action

The United States shares many issues with other countries. The World Economic Forum summarizes these challenges in table 5.1. But, some other countries have chosen to tackle these issues. This shows us that the Guaranteed Retirement Account model can work because we have seen similar models work around the world.

AUSTRALIA'S SUPERANNUATION GUARANTEE

Retirement observers perceive Australia's Superannuation Guarantee[1]—a mandated savings system with similarities to our model for Guaranteed Retirement Accounts—as a potential road map for the United States.[2] And for good reason: it has worked spectacularly well in helping people accumulate assets.

As recently as the 1980s, Australia's retirement system resembled the U.S. system today. Pension plans covered less than half of the workforce, and Australia had an aging

Table 5.1 Common Challenges of Retirement Planning

Increasing life expectancies and lower birth rates	Low levels of financial literacy
Population over 65 will increase from 600 million today to 2.1 billion in 2050	Globally, the majority of citizens are not able to correctly answer simple financial literacy questions
8 workers per retiree today, compared to 4 per retiree in 2050	Increasingly important given trend towards self-directed nature of pensions
Lack of easy access to pensions	**Inadequate savings rates**
Over 50% of workers globally are in the informal/ unorganized sector	Contributions to DC plans typically significantly lower than 10–15% target
48% of retirement age population do not receive a pension	Saving rates are not aligned with individuals' expectations for retirement income – puts at risk the credibility of the whole pension system
Long term low growth environment	**High degree of individual responsibility to manage pension**
Future investment returns expected to be ~5% (equities) and ~3% (bonds) below historic averages	Define contribution plans (individually managed) account for over 50% of pension assets
Returns misaligned with benefit projects and individual expectations	Individuals are required to be their own investment manager, actuary and insurer
High costs eroding invest-ment growth	

Source: World Economic Forum, *We'll Live to 100—How Can We Afford It?* https://www.weforum.org/whitepapers/we-ll-live-to-100-how-can-we-afford-it.

population.[3] Many Australians were falling short in retirement, just as millions of American seniors are falling short today.[4]

In response, Australia pursued a then-novel solution: a retirement savings mandate. In 1992, it implemented its national superannuation savings program. Today, employers automatically contribute 9.5 percent of each worker's salary to a long-term retirement savings account. (The percentage is set to rise to 10 percent in 2021, and to 12 percent in 2025.) On a voluntary basis, workers are encouraged to contribute extra if they can.[5]

It is pertinent to note that the Australian contribution level far outstrips the GRA's proposed 3 percent minimum, that the mandate falls entirely on the employer, and that the program has in no way damaged the Australian economy or inhibited growth. In fact, more than two decades after it began, the model is a clear success. Before the system was enacted, only 23 percent of Australia's low-income construction workers and government clerks had retirement pensions. Today, *all* workers are covered by a retirement plan. User satisfaction is high and on the rise.[6] The program currently has almost AU\$2 trillion in savings, nearly as much as the country's total gross domestic product.[7]

It is not a perfect system. Upon retirement, Australian savers can structure their benefit as a lump sum, a phased withdrawal, or an annuity. The resulting "lack of annuitization makes older Australians heavily exposed to longevity, inflation, and investment risks."[8]

Despite this weakness, however, Australia far exceeds most of the world in promoting a secure retirement. On key measures of effectiveness, sustainability, and integrity, its system trails only those of Denmark and the Netherlands.[9] By contrast, as measured by the Melbourne Mercer Global Pension Index Survey, the U.S. retirement system lags behind, on a tier with Mexico and South Africa. The United States ranks below the median of other countries for "adequacy" and "integrity," although it ranks above the median for "sustainability."[10]

RETIREMENT PLANS IN THE UNITED STATES

In the United States, states are the laboratories for democracy and for innovative social policy. As of late 2016, with U.S. federal action still missing in action, more than twenty-six states had acted to address the retirement crisis. A few began moving toward a GRA-style model, and Oregon and Illinois enacted plans for mandated retirement savings, but these plans include an opt-out provision.

The Obama administration removed a number of regulatory hurdles to support this approach. "We want to do everything we can to encourage more states to take this step," President Obama said in 2015. "We've got to make it easier for people to save for retirement."[11]

One regulatory rule, adopted in August 2016, freed state-sponsored individual retirement accounts from the Employment Retirement Income Security Act (ERISA) if they had equivalent oversight. The rule was enacted over objections of the investment and insurance industries,[12] which feared competition from state-run, low-cost alternatives for retirement savings. Unfortunately, in March 2017, with the backing of the Trump administration, the Republican Congress voted to overturn the Obama rule. Despite this setback, a number of states and three large cities—New York, Philadelphia, and Seattle—continue to advance their solutions to the retirement crisis.

It is important to remember that states and cities are being forced to act because of the lack of federal legislation, and these smaller systems cannot benefit from the economies of scale available to a national model. Nor can they create comparable tax breaks to incentivize savings, make retirement plans portable across state lines, or provide secure backing for a guaranty of the annuities. Finally, they cannot efficiently utilize the Social Security Administration payment system.[13] Nonetheless, these experiments can make a difference. As David John, an AARP expert, noted in the *New York Times*, "We know these plans work, because people are 15 times more likely to save by having access to payroll deduction."[14]

At the same time, it must be recognized that coordinated regulation, management, asset pooling, and risk management of retirement accounts would be far more effective on a national scale. The immediacy of our retirement crisis demands a national solution.

As noted in appendix B, many proposals are now being put forward regarding universal retirement accounts. But none of these plans are as detailed or as expansive as the GRA in identifying and addressing an array of fundamental problems.

To solve the retirement crisis, we need new federal legislation and national leadership.

6

WHY NOT JUST EXPAND
SOCIAL SECURITY?

Americans Need a Universal Pension System

Social Security was enacted in 1935, and it has served as the foundation for retirement security for most Americans ever since its introduction. If anything, Americans want more of it. Based on recent polling data, a large majority (84 percent) believes that Social Security fails to provide adequate income for retirees.[1] Resistance to reducing benefits can be found across the political spectrum, from the very liberal (66 percent) to the very conservative (59 percent). Most voters oppose means testing, a rise in the retirement age, or any other form of benefit cut.[2]

What people want instead are policies for a more secure retirement for working Americans. The National Academy for Social Insurance found that 75 percent of those polled support an increase in Social Security benefits to that end. A large majority (82 percent) support the preservation of Social Security by increasing the taxes paid by wealthier Americans. When presented with reforms to increase tax revenues and generate larger benefits, 71 percent are in favor of doing so.[3]

The polling data are clear. Americans are worried about retirement security and whether Social Security will even be there for them. Most want the program to be expanded or supplemented.

Historically, however, Social Security was not meant to fund retirement by itself. It was designed as a safety net for individuals facing poverty in old age. Middle-class households were assumed to have pensions and personal savings on top of Social Security to help maintain their lifestyles once they were no longer working. That is the pillar we must restore today.

It is important to note that the share of preretirement earnings replaced by Social Security has steadily fallen since the 1980s. We believe it is essential for Congress to ensure the solvency of Social Security for generations to come, but even a fully funded Social Security is not enough. We must do more to provide retirement security for all Americans.

A Guaranteed Retirement Account (GRA) system, working in concert with Social Security, is a more practical option for America's future retirees than a sizable Social Security expansion. Let us count the ways.

First, expanding Social Security would require raising taxes or increasing the deficit, or both. The GRA model, by contrast, is budget neutral. Employee contributions are completely or partly subsidized by a tax credit, and these credits are paid for by eliminating tax breaks for higher-income earners. The net cost to the U.S. Treasury is zero.

Second, unlike Social Security, GRAs rely on actual cash in each person's individually owned retirement savings account. When this real capital is pooled in large GRA accounts, plan managers are able to choose high-performing investments, which will close the retirement wealth gap without adding costs for anyone.

Third, Social Security is an entitlement that redistributes savings based on income. Expanding the program would certainly lift up the poorest elderly Americans. But no proposed expansion of Social Security would do enough to replace the 70 percent of middle-class wages needed to sustain a preretirement lifestyle for these workers. GRAs are add-on accounts to provide a secure and comfortable retirement across the income spectrum.

Finally, there is no political consensus on either goals or fixes for Social Security. In the prevailing political environment, reaching a consensus would seem improbable, if not impossible. GRAs work largely within the existing system to deliver retirement security. Based on many meetings with politicians from both parties, regulators, CEOs, labor representatives, and asset managers, we believe a broad consensus can be reached in support of Guaranteed Retirement Accounts.

No country has a universal, pay-as-you go pension system similar to Social Security that affords the middle class a secure retirement. Greece tried to do so in the post–World War II period and failed. More recently, Spain did the same, and its system is failing as well. These programs place unsustainable burdens on younger workers to fund retirement for a rapidly growing elderly population.

Models that mix a government-run, pay-as-you-go element with an advance-funded program for accumulation, investment, and annuitization have seen more success. These hybrid systems—in the Netherlands, Australia, and Denmark—are best-in-class for retirement security and sustainable design.

People are aware of the retirement crisis. It will quickly become very personal. When they see that there is an effective solution, they will demand it and not worry ab out philosophical battles. Our plan will help, but for many Americans—especially those retiring in the next decade—there will still be plenty of need and pressure to reform Social Security, the bedrock on which our GRA plan is built. Both programs are needed to provide retirement security for all Americans.

7

GROWING SUPPORT FROM THE AMERICAN PEOPLE AND A MANDATE FOR CONGRESS

We have put a lot of thought into our plan for Guaranteed Retirement Accounts (GRAs). We have considered the eventualities that need to be addressed, the protections and guarantees that need to be put in place, the costs that need to be accounted for—and the political ramifications that must be acknowledged. Retirement is an issue fraught with controversy; it is easy to become dispirited by the scope of the challenge facing the United States today. Nonetheless, we believe GRAs are politically viable for a number of reasons.

First, the GRA plan does not touch any third rails. It does not alter Social Security or force abandonment of the existing 401(k) and IRA systems. It does, however, incentivize a shift to GRAs by ending the tax breaks for these old plans. The GRA is simply a more effective alternative. It relieves our welfare programs from undue strain and frees revenue for other pressing needs. It offers an actionable solution to a critical threat to the economic future of the United States.

Second, the U.S. retirement crisis will be a huge political issue—with dire consequences for elected officials—if it is *not* addressed. Studies show that retirement worries pervade all segments of American society, including those who have relatively high incomes or guaranteed pension plans. If implemented, the GRA solution will have a resounding impact on well over half of all working Americans, including those most at risk of poverty in retirement. Few significant policy reform proposals can say as much.

Third, and perhaps most important, the American people are clamoring for a national retirement solution. According to a 2017 survey, 88 percent of Americans "believe that the nation faces a retirement crisis"; 86 percent want "national policy makers to give more attention to retirement issues"; and 72 percent say they "would be willing to take less in salary increases in exchange for guaranteed income in retirement."[1]

These results are echoed by Gallup, which finds that retirement is American's number one financial worry. Most (76 percent) retirees rely on Social Security as a major source of income. In 2014, 59 percent said they were very or moderately worried about having enough money to retire. Over the last three years, Gallup polling has consistently shown that three of four Americans are concerned about the Social Security system.

These numbers do not favor the status quo. Nor do they suggest that Americans are unrealistic in their approach to retirement. The American people understand that change is necessary, and they are prepared to embrace it.

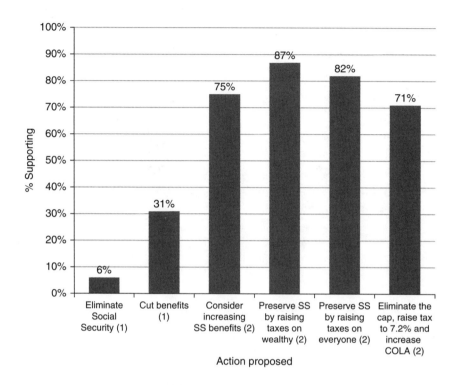

Figure 7.1 Voters want to expand social security.

Source: (1) Pew Research (2014). *Political polarization in the American public.* (2) Tucker, J., Reno, V. & Bethel, T. (2013). *Strengthening social security: what do Americans want?*. National Academy of Social Insurance.

The retirement crisis is looming, and the public appetite for strong federal action is apparent. The time for action has come (figure 7.1).

Independent research shows overwhelming support for GRAs (figure 7.2). What makes the GRA so appealing? In particular, people like the fact that both employer and

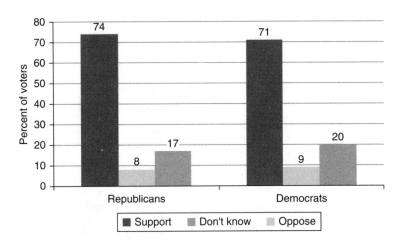

Figure 7.2 Respondents across the political spectrum supported GRAs.

employee contribute, and that a GRA plan follows savers from job to job, with no worries about rollovers or reinvestment and penalties. Respondents also like the plan's guaranteed monthly payments in retirement.

Pensions may be hard to find these days, but they are still very much in vogue!

GUARANTEED RETIREMENT ACCOUNTS CAN HOLD BIPARTISAN APPEAL BECAUSE THEY . . .

- Help working Americans by providing retirement plans to 85 million people without one
- Address a massive issue that cuts across demographics.
- Do not create a new entitlement or bureaucracy.
- Do not increase the federal deficit.

- Foster individual accounts with personal ownership and oversight, immune from government diversion.
- Are virtually costless for most individuals.
- Facilitate capital formation to spur economic growth.
- Are simple for small businesses to implement.

FOCUS GROUP POLLING ON THE GUARANTEED RETIREMENT PLAN

An independent consulting firm, Quadrant Strategies, which specializes in qualitative and quantitative research, was retained by independent third parties to research the GRA plan. Quadrant constructed six randomly selected groups of individuals recruited from databases of tens of thousands of people in each city. The groups were identified by their age and political leanings. The three geographical locations were Boston, on December 12, 2016; Metro Detroit, on December 14, 2016; and Atlanta, on December 15, 2016.

The locations were chosen because of the high concentration of key political subgroups in each market. The political leanings of the voters in each geographical location were chosen for particular reasons. The "liberal progressives" were interviewed in Boston because of the initial hypothesis that left-leaning voters would be most supportive of the GRA. The suburban Rust Belt Trump voters were interviewed in Detroit because of their emergence as the decisive segment of the voting population in the 2016 presidential election.

(continued)

And the conservatives in Atlanta were interviewed because of the historical opposition to new laws among right-leaning Americans. Two groups were interviewed in each of the three places. In Boston and Atlanta, the near-retirement-age group consisted of those between the ages of fifty-five and seventy and the younger millennial group consisted of those between the ages of eighteen and thirty-four. In Detroit, the older age group consisted of those between the ages of forty-five and sixty, and the younger group consisted of those between the ages of eighteen and forty. The similar split age groups in each market were chosen because of the hypothesis that younger workers (those furthest away from retirement) and older workers (those almost at retirement age) would be the most resistant to a new retirement program.

Each group spent an hour and a half with an expert moderator. Panelists first were asked to read and discuss questions that tested their overall perceptions of their own and the nation's retirement crisis. The next set of questions was about a proposal called "the guaranteed retirement account," which is described in this book. Quadrant used the results of these focus groups to devise a questionnaire they sent to thousands of online interviewees. The people chosen to receive the survey were selected at random from a large national respondent panel, which is compiled, maintained, and curated by one of the nation's leading market research sample vendors. Out of the 5,750 people who responded to the survey invitation, 3,000 both qualified to take the survey (maintaining a sample representative of the U.S. population) and fully completed the survey. The survey was conducted using best-practice market research and statistical methods.

8

THE EMPLOYER'S STAKE
IN RETIREMENT REFORM

Employers are at the heart of the U.S. retirement system. Every business owner benefits when the money he or she pays for workers' retirement is efficiently used. Yet the concerns employers have around retirement issues are poorly understood by policy makers. In Chapter 4, we discussed how the Guaranteed Retirement Account affects employers. Here we make a case that all businesses have a stake in the GRA.

Defined-contribution plans supplanted the defined-benefit system because employers were eager to avoid volatile future liabilities. Most business owners cannot afford to offer defined-benefit pensions when their competitors do not do the same. Even a defined-contribution plan such as a 401(k) can be discouraging to administer with its welter of regulations. For small-business owners, particularly those with low-income employees, the time, effort, costs, and liability of a retirement plan often outweigh the best of intentions.

At the same time, employers know that their employees are anxious. Every employer knows a worker who is heading toward poverty. Many employers *want* to do better by their employees but feel that their hands are tied. We do not believe our retirement crisis is the fault of employers or workers; this crisis has come about due to a flawed system subsidized by skewed tax deductions that were created by Congress.

A Guaranteed Retirement Account would allow employers to adopt an automated payroll deduction retirement plan, a far less onerous burden than sponsoring a plan themselves. Many employers find 401(k)s impractical because they lack economies of scale: the costs are too high and the administrative burdens are daunting. Under a higher-performing GRA plan, most administrative and fiduciary responsibilities shift from employers to the federal government and professional, certified GRA managers. With a GRA plan, employers can do the right thing without fear of hurting their business.

As matters stand, 401(k)s are expensive to administer and lackluster in performance. By and large, they fail to guarantee a lifetime income. They distract employers from their core business and carry fiduciary risk.

Finally, employers sponsoring a 401(k) plan are bedeviled by how to handle workers who change jobs and are disinclined or unable to consolidate their retirement savings in a new employer plan or IRA. Both worker and employer face discouraging complexities in this process.

Contrast this distressing situation with a workplace implementing a Guaranteed Retirement Account. Thanks to

EMPLOYERS WANT MANDATED SAVINGS

In 2010, a national magazine asked Teresa Ghilarducci to speak to their annual conference. She made a deal: she would speak if they allowed her to survey her audience of 250 employer plan sponsors and advisors. The survey ranged from employers' views of the current defined-contribution system to possible alternatives.

Here is what Teresa found:

- Employers and plan sponsors worried that their employees were ill-prepared for retirement. They believed people do not save enough due in part to poor spending habits. But the larger problem, they believed, was a system that fails to provide the necessary tools for retirement security.

- Of the firms choosing not to sponsor or expand retirement plans, a plurality (44 percent) said the plans are too expensive. Others cited administrative burdens and regulatory complexity, 22 percent and 21 percent, respectively.

- When polled on the most appropriate way for the United States to address increasing retirement costs in an aging society, a majority (52 percent) chose "mandating that people save more" over "raising the retirement age" (29 percent), "raising taxes" (10 percent), or "cutting benefits" (8 percent). Nearly two-thirds (63 percent) of respondents favored mandating that people save more to supplement Social Security.

a GRA annuity, the employee has a genuine opportunity for a stable retirement—without creating an unfunded liability for the employer. And by barring early fund withdrawal, the GRA eliminates the temptation for workers to cash out. In addition, employers would no longer be required to manage residual 401(k) accounts for departed employees, a bête noire for any business.

Every employer gains a valuable human resource planning tool if workers know what they will have when they retire—or what they stand to gain by extending their working lives and claiming Social Security benefits later. In addition, if Medicare is the first payer rather than the second, as the GRA model stipulates, employers would save thousands of dollars annually on health care premiums for each employee over age sixty-five.

Employers cannot remain silent; they must join others in addressing this issue. The problems are real, serious, and complex, but they also are solvable. We have had decades to observe both private sector retirement plans and public programs. We have gained a solid understanding of what works and what does not. Our intent is not to reinvent the wheel but to move forward with an innovative and thoughtful package of reforms—some traditionally favored by liberals, others by conservatives, and many by both.

No one-size-fits-all solution will guarantee retirement security for all. Varying income levels and individual situations demand a variety of approaches. But one point is clear and indisputable: every American should be able to retire with dignity. The GRA is a promising first step toward making that aspiration a reality.

9

CONCLUSION

It is not rash speculation to say that poverty looms for millions of our elderly. The demographics, cost inflation, and savings and income trends are all known. If we do nothing, our retirement crisis will become a catastrophe.

The situation may be daunting, but it is by no measure insurmountable. We have the tools to solve the problem. We just need to put them into action.

In fact, we have a solution that is remarkably simple and effective. By enacting a national system of Guaranteed Retirement Accounts, we can secure a comfortable retirement for most Americans. We can deliver a higher rate of return on workers' savings. We can annuitize benefits to provide steady income, no matter how long people live. And we can do all of this in a way that requires little or no additional government spending and virtually no new bureaucracy.

We believe we can even win bipartisan support. All that is missing is the political will to tackle this crisis while we still can.

Will we start while there is still time? Or will we wait for the chilling statistical predictions to become real-life human tragedies?

If we act now, we will have time to build up savings gradually. The required sacrifices will be relatively modest. If we wait, the costs will be enormous.

It is rare that a program can be simultaneously sweeping and deficit neutral, visionary yet practical. But the retirement program we have presented to you here is designed to do all of that.

Guaranteed Retirement Accounts will afford Americans a stronger, more stable retirement—and offer us a chance to set this country on a trajectory for a more sustainable future for generations to come.

QUESTIONS AND ANSWERS ON THE GUARANTEED RETIREMENT ACCOUNT

Do GRAs work for people already approaching retirement age?

Because the GRA relies on a lifetime of saving and higher investment returns, this model will be most effective for individuals with several decades to save for retirement. That said, everyone wins by saving more and earning higher returns in advance of retirement, no matter their age. Even people in their fifties can benefit. If they save effectively for ten or twelve years, they can use those savings in retirement to delay taking Social Security benefits, which translates to a larger monthly check down the road. And when they do start receiving Social Security, their GRAs supplement and fortify their retirement income. The added money put aside and the accumulated return on those savings rewards people for staying in the workforce a little longer. The extra benefits from as many as eight additional years of work can increase retirement income 70 percent, providing a far more comfortable retirement.

Are low-wage workers treated fairly under this plan?

The GRA plan is much fairer to low-wage workers than is the status quo. For nearly all households at or below the median U.S. salary, it guarantees a significant boost to retirement savings at no cost.

Our plan directly supports low-wage workers in two ways. The GRA's refundable tax credit offsets a worker's contribution by up to $600 each year, a formula considerably more equitable than the current tax deduction model. Second, it establishes a floor for employer contributions at fifteen cents per hour, further augmenting low-wage workers' retirement savings.

Will people be vulnerable in a market downturn?

Under the GRA plan, the government safeguards all retirees' mandated principal contributions in full. Even if they stop working during a major market downturn, their retirement savings are protected. In addition, the principal protection guarantee entails a nominal cost or none at all (see appendix A).

Over the long haul, it is highly likely that GRAs can earn at least a 6 or 7 percent nominal return. In most cases, they will return much more than the sum contributed, regardless of short-term economic conditions. This contrasts with 401(k)s, which were decimated in the 2007–2010 recession.

Could the 3 percent savings mandate be raised in the future?

Retirement savings calculators, based on moderate assumptions for rates of return over a forty-year career, suggest that people consistently saving 3 percent of income will have enough to maintain their quality of life in retirement. However, if future circumstances indicate that greater baseline savings are necessary or desirable, policy makers will have the option to increase the savings mandate. In other countries, where similar plans have proven highly popular, contribution rates have risen over time.

Do savers legally own their GRAs?

Yes. The money in savers' GRAs is truly theirs; ownership is legally explicit. GRAs cannot be garnished by a creditor as loan collateral or tapped by government for other uses.

Can heirs inherit a deceased partner's GRA?

Regardless of whether individuals die before or after their GRA accounts becomes an annuity, our plan ensures that the surviving spouse is cared for. In the event of a death before annuitization, the spouse and other heirs inherit the GRA in full, as with any savings account. GRA annuities are calculated by household, factoring in family size and longevity assumptions. Deaths occurring after annuitization have no effect on the surviving spouse's GRA benefit, making it one less worry during a painful time.

How will the plan support retirees who have children with disabilities?

For retirees with long-term dependents, GRAs can be modified for additional annuitants. Monthly annuity payments are reduced as more people in the household are covered to keep the value of the annuity in equilibrium with the GRA balance at the time of retirement.

Can someone withdraw from a GRA in case of an emergency?

To function well, the GRA model must work the same way as a defined-benefit pension plan and prohibit early withdrawals.

Was there a role for the disbanded myRA accounts under the Retirement Savings Plan?

There was a role for something like a myRA program which was limited to small amounts (less than $15,000). That is not nearly enough to fund a secure retirement.

However, something like a myRA program is a good option for people wanting a rainy day fund. It could coexist well with the Retirement Savings Plan, where savings are protected until retirement. Coupled with the GRA, the myRA program could have been beneficial, since people won't be able to withdraw from their GRA in case of an emergency.

Is it fair to encourage people to work longer?

Participation in the labor force is, of course, purely voluntary. The GRA plan simply gives older workers who might wish to work longer a benefit for doing so.

What is truly unfair is leaving Americans with no effective means to save for retirement, then expecting them to get by for decades after they stop working or to seek work well into old age. That is our current system. The GRA model recognizes a new reality. At a time when people are living longer than ever, their retirement savings must last longer as well. Workers who choose to delay retirement gain more time to accumulate savings and to allow those savings to earn returns and grow. Up to age seventy, their Social Security benefit increases with each month it is deferred. These workers also will be stretching their savings over fewer years in retirement.

Is there a risk that companies now offering high-quality retirement plans will reduce their benefits in switching to a GRA plan?

Companies converting from 401(k)s to GRAs are prohibited from reducing benefits for two years. Any retirement benefits offered today are strictly voluntary, so it is reasonable to assume that employers will continue to be motivated to maintain benefit levels.

Who is responsible for investing the funds? Are GRAs a windfall for Wall Street?

Individual savers choose their own pension manager, based on fees and investment performance, and there will be many from which to choose. The managers determine asset allocation and select the money managers who make the actual investments. As federally licensed and regulated GRA fiduciaries, they provide a layer of protection between the worker and Wall Street, a buffer that is missing with 401(k)s or IRAs. In addition, each pension manager reports to an independent board of trustees.

At the program's outset, the default pension manager is the Federal Thrift Savings Plan or the pension fund in the worker's state of residence. But a wide range of institutions will be able to manage GRAs, from traditional money management firms and mutual fund companies to government entities. Accounts are fully portable, and assets will transfer from one manager to another without fees or penalties.

A few states have enacted their own retirement plans. Is that enough?

Although the efforts by individual states are laudable, the only real solution for the retirement crisis is a national one. Retirement savings must be portable across state lines and governed by consistent guidelines. The GRA plan redeploys federal tax deductions into federal tax credits to subsidize lower-income savers. In addition, it gains efficiency by using the Social Security infrastructure for administration. Finally, national economies of scale make the system cheaper to administer and more likely to generate a higher return for savers.

Does the combination of mandating GRAs and ending tax breaks for 401(k)s and IRAs take retirement savings decisions away from individuals?

No. Each individual controls his or her own account. For too long, the American people have been left on their own to prepare for retirement, which is why so few of us are prepared today. The research and empirical evidence make clear that only a savings mandate can solve the problem facing us today.

Would it be more practical to simply expand Social Security?

Social Security provides workers with a base level of security, and we do not propose changing that. The GRA is a supplement, not a replacement. Social Security was designed as a modest safety net for those facing poverty in old age. It was never meant to guarantee a middle-class retirement, and it is not the best vehicle to do so moving forward.

Won't the principal protection guarantee put taxpayers on the hook if the financial markets crash as they did in 2008?

The guarantee's liability for the federal government is negligible.[1] In fact, over a twenty-five-year period, no professionally managed pension fund has ever failed to generate a positive return. It is highly unlikely that the government will incur any significant cost from the principal protection guarantee. (Accordingly, the guarantee has *de minimis* actual economic value; see appendix A.) However, the cost of the guarantee will be scored by the nonpartisan Congressional Budget Office, and a modest premium will be charged to offset that cost. We believe that cost will begin very small and decline to nearly zero over time.

The guarantee is a floor under every GRA account. Upon retirement, workers are assured of having a balance no less than their total in principal contributions. This minimum balance would be used solely for the government's computation of minimum monthly payments on the date they retire, when their GRA rolls into an annuity.

The guarantee's main value is psychological, to provide savers with peace of mind. But if even this unlikely and modest cost is more than legislators wish to bear, GRA holders could pay a nominal insurance premium. In any event, this provision has no effect on investment risk or return. A GRA portfolio is managed independently, without regard to the guarantee.

APPENDIX A

THE COST OF A PRINCIPAL PROTECTION GUARANTEE

To test the potential costs of a federal government guarantee that each GRA saver will get back at least as much as he or she contributes, we have constructed a series of simulations for future return scenarios. Our research unequivocally found that a principal protection guarantee poses no significant financial risk to taxpayers.[*] In particular, our analysis revealed the following:

1. It is unlikely that the government's principal protection guarantee ever would be triggered. Over the past seventy years, no forty-year period would have put the guarantee into play.
2. Even if the guarantee were to be triggered, costs would be minimal and could be covered easily by a nominal, one-time, upfront fee of fifteen dollars on each GRA, or by a modest annual insurance premium.
3. The principal protection guarantee would be most likely to be invoked in the program's infancy, when savers have been contributing for just a few years. In this scenario, any

potential costs would be minimal because the younger GRA holder would have a much smaller amount at risk. The potential costs grow slightly for the first five years, then begins to decline with each subsequent year. Once the GRA program has passed its transitional implementation stage, maintaining the guarantee almost certainly will be costless.

In this appendix, we consider these findings one at a time. This analytical work uses a 6.75 percent return assumption. We believe anything in the 6 to 7 percent range is reasonable, although for the most part our examples have used a slightly lower 6.5 percent assumed return.

1 IT IS UNLIKELY THAT THE PRINCIPAL PROTECTION GUARANTEE WILL BE TRIGGERED

To understand why the principal protection guarantee is unlikely to come into play, consider how the accounts are structured. Workers cannot withdraw funds until retirement. Accounts are pooled and invested in balanced portfolios that are not correlated with one another. These larger, pooled accounts enjoy lower fees and advantages of scale, including superior diversification options and access to alternative investments. As GRAs are aggregated on a national scale, risks are diffused as well.

To measure the size and likelihood of risks posed to taxpayers, we constructed a series of Monte Carlo simulations. Our analysis found that the probability of the guarantee being called after forty years ranges from 0.1 percent to 0.4 percent.[1] In every simulation, the cost of the guarantee could be covered by the fee reserve (discussed later).

Table A.1 compares our conservative baseline scenario for GRA returns with actual returns over recent seventy- and twenty-five-year periods.

Since the period ending in 1985, rolling forty-year average annual returns on pension funds have consistently ranged from 7 percent to 10 percent. In other words, even a 6.5 percent guarantee would never have been called. The chances of a zero percent guarantee—the equivalent of principal protection—seems remote, even in a worst-case scenario.

Consider the period from 1969 to 2008, which ended in a global financial crisis. In 2008, when portfolio values dropped

Table A.1 Comparison of Assumed GRA Returns and Volatility with Historical Actuals

	Returns	Standard Deviation
2015–2055 (Baseline GRA prediction)	6.75%	11%
1945–2015	8.7%	11.4%
1990–2015	8.9%	10.3%

Source: MSCI Analytics. "InvestorForce Report," MSCI.com, https://www.msci.com /documents/1296102/1636401/InvestorForce_Report.pdf/1b6f2b80-dbfe-4f69 -995a-4e2131fbc2fa.

by 25 percent, the forty-year average return fell by only 1.5 percent. GRA savers annuitizing that year would have earned close to an 8 percent annual return. Pension funds would have had to lose 88 percent in 2008 to push lifetime average returns into negative territory.

2 EVEN IF THE PRINCIPAL PROTECTION GUARANTEE IS TRIGGERED, COSTS WILL BE MINIMAL AND EASILY COVERED BY A NEGLIGIBLE FEE ON ALL GRAS

It is relatively straightforward to calculate the costs in the unlikely circumstance that the principal protection guarantee is triggered.

Let's use a saver who is earning $52,000 a year, a point between the median and the average annual earnings of a full-time American worker, to illustrate this point. Assuming a forty-year career and 2 percent annual wage growth, this individual would cumulatively contribute $98,000 to his or her GRA. The expected portfolio value, based on a 6.75 percent annual return, would be $393,000.

To insure against the extremely unlikely event of negative GRA returns over forty years, the government could impose a onetime fee of fifteen dollars for each new GRA member—our calculation of the present expected value of the principal protection guarantee. Our proposal does not necessarily recommend the levy; it merely illustrates the guarantee's theoretical cost.

Through the fifteen dollar fee, the reserve fund would receive $2.4 billion in the first year and $8 billion over the program's first forty years. At the forty-year mark, accrued at a long-term, risk-free rate, the reserve fund would be $21 billion, large enough to cover more than half of all loss scenarios in our Monte Carlo simulations. This lowers the probability of a taxpayer obligation to an infinitesimal 0.001 percent.

3 ONCE THE PROGRAM IS MATURE, MAINTAINING THE GUARANTEE ALMOST CERTAINLY WILL BE COSTLESS

The risk of a reserve fund shortfall is unevenly distributed over the life of the program. In fact, the only net deficit scenarios occur in the early transitional period when the GRA system is instituted, when large numbers of participants will have enrolled mid-career. Even in these unlikely scenarios, taxpayers' exposure is small, for a simple reason: people make fewer contributions over a shorter time frame. If a GRA had been introduced in 2004, for example, 1.7 million workers who retired in 2008, would have claimed benefits under the guarantee in the Great Financial Crisis that year. But the shortfall, even then, would have been relatively small, just over $1 billion, because the median participant would have been exposed to losses on only $4,800 invested.

Similarly, if a GRA were instituted today, risks associated with large drops in the market value of worker portfolios

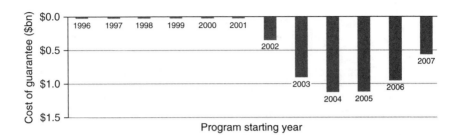

Figure A.1 Projected cost of guarantee starting 2016 for each cohort if there are 6.75% annual returns until retirement year and then a 25% decline.

would be greatest in the first five years, then begin to wane (see table B.2). After ten years, there is essentially zero risk. Assuming a 6.75 percent average annual return for the first four years, followed by a 25 percent market collapse in 2021, the median portfolio for an individual retiring that year would be down only $1,100.

In this scenario, the guarantee's total cost would be $2.5 billion, less than the value of fees collected to that point. In *every* scenario, including a 25 percent market drop in the first year of implementation, the buffer would be large enough to cover losses without a need for government intervention.

PROJECTED COST OF GUARANTEE BEGINNING IN 2016 FOR EACH COHORT, ASSUMING 6.75 PERCENT ANNUAL RETURNS UNTIL RETIREMENT YEAR AND THEN A 25 PERCENT DECLINE

As figure A.2 illustrates, there would only have been any exposure if the GRA had been started within six years of the

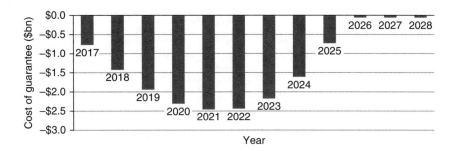

Figure A.2 Cost of principal protection guarantee for the cohort retiring during the 2008 financial crisis (1.7 million people) by hypothetical GRA starting next year.

financial crisis, and even then, the total costs would never have been much above $1 billion.

ADDITIONAL RESEARCH: THE LOW-RISK POTENTIAL OF GUARANTEES

In analyzing costing guarantees, it may be tempting to fall back on standard financial engineering textbook approaches, which tend to project higher prices through option pricing techniques. Although these techniques are appropriate in financial markets, they are less useful in estimating the cost of government guarantees.

- A government guarantee on a retirement account is not a pure financial transaction between independent market participants. A government guarantee is a transaction among all workers facilitated by the government.
- As such, the option price is not the "value of resources foregone" by society, as claimed by a 2016 Brookings Institution paper.[2]

A broad body of research supports our conclusions. Alicia Munnell et al. found no significant risk in a 2 to 3 percent nominal return guarantee.[3] (Again, our guarantee is predicated on a zero percent return.) Stubbs used Monte Carlo simulations and eighty years of market returns to model a 3.5 percent real return guarantee. Assuming a balanced portfolio, he found little to no risk of falling short.[4]

Olivia Mitchell argues that a return guarantee is irresponsible, but her context is fundamentally different.[5] Mitchell's research focuses on guarantees of pure equity portfolios and at much higher levels than our GRA proposal. In fact, Lachance and Mitchell maintain that the cost of providing principal protection for a 50:50 equity/bond split portfolio would be less than one dollar per account.[6]

Notwithstanding all of this, our plan assumes that the cost of the guarantee will be scored by the Congressional Budget Office and that a modest premium will be assessed on each account to defray that cost. For the reasons described here, the premium should decline to nearly zero over time.

CONCLUSION

In summary, the risks of a government principal protection guarantee for individual retirement accounts are minimal, and the peace of mind provided to savers is crucial. In every scenario, the GRA system is a cost-effective way to guarantee a secure pension for every American worker.

APPENDIX B

GRAs VERSUS OTHER POLICY SOLUTIONS

In recognition of the onrushing retirement crisis, numerous policy proposals have surfaced at both the state and federal levels.[1] In 2009, the Obama administration proposed an "Auto IRA," which failed to advance in Congress. Meanwhile, at least fourteen state governments have considered various types of retirement plans for private sector workers. The states' efforts to innovate—and to compensate for inadequate retirement plan coverage—reflects the need for a federal solution. As the history of Social Security demonstrates, innovation at the state level often informs and shapes federal programs.

OBAMA ADMINISTRATION'S AUTO IRA

This proposal aimed to benefit workers who lacked access to a retirement plan at work. It would have required employers without a retirement plan to enroll their employees in a direct-deposit IRA account compatible with existing direct-deposit payroll systems.[2] Under the proposal, 3 percent of each paycheck would be deposited into a Roth IRA, to which contributions are made with after-tax dollars. Withdrawals would be tax free for account holders age fifty-nine and a half or older on accounts held for at least five years.[3]

Obama's Auto IRA initiative also proposed to expand retirement savings incentives for working families. It would have modified the existing saver's credit to provide a one-time 50 percent match on the first $1,000 of retirement savings for families earning less than $65,000 a year. To ensure that savings incentives are fair to all workers, the credit would have been fully refundable.[4]

Auto IRA Advantages

- Contributors to Auto IRA accounts could benefit from the saver's credit, a contribution for low- and middle-income workers saving for retirement. In this case, the federal government would partially offset the cost of the saver's IRA contribution.
- Automatic enrollment is of proven effectiveness in helping workers save for retirement. The Auto IRA would bring more workers into retirement savings programs.

Disadvantages

- The proposal did not advance in Congress.
- Employees can opt out or withdraw from Auto IRA accounts before retirement, jeopardizing retirement savings.

- The saver's credit requires more than $50 billion in government tax expenditures, assuming it is to be refundable and income limits are increased.[5]
- IRA returns are generally low.
- Savings are not annuitized into lifelong income.

OBAMA ADMINISTRATION'S myRA

After the Obama administration's original Auto IRA was rejected by Congress, the United States Treasury developed a retirement account plan entitled "myRA." It was a Roth IRA that allowed individual savers to contribute up to $5,500 annually to their retirement account.

These contributions were invested in U.S. government securities, which averaged an annual return of 3.19 percent over the ten years ending in December 2014.[6] Employers were not required to directly administer or contribute to the accounts, only to facilitate them by deducting contributions from paychecks through direct deposit.

To avoid competition with financial services firms, the U.S. Treasury directly administered myRA accounts in cooperation with private sector banks. The accounts were rolled over into private sector IRAs once the account balance exceeded the $15,000 myRA maximum amount, or after thirty years, whichever came first.[7]

Advantages

- These accounts are designed to increase retirement savings.

- Individuals contributing to myRAs were potentially eligible for the saver's credit.
- Workers were shielded from investment and market risks by investing in U.S. Treasury securities, which guarantee against loss of principal.

Disadvantages

- President Trump eliminated myRAs as competition to retail managers in Summer 2017.
- myRA accounts were voluntary for both employer and employee. Without mandates, most taxpayers were unlikely to participate, especially lower-income individuals.[8]
- The contribution cap of $15,000 may have inhibited significant savings.
- myRAs converted into commercial IRAs that typically had high fees.
- The return on U.S. government securities was low.
- No provision for annuities existed.

Overall, myRA accounts were a positive first step to expand savings. But without automatic enrollment, and given their low cap, they could not have effectively addressed retirement needs.

THE SECURE CHOICE RETIREMENT SAVINGS PROGRAM

Secure Choice Pensions (SCPs) are state-level proposals to provide retirement security by requiring certain employers to make payroll deductions for savings in Roth IRAs.[9]

A handful of states—Illinois, Massachusetts, Oregon, California, Maryland, and Connecticut—have made efforts toward researching and implementing automatic payroll deduction retirement plans. Participants would be fully and immediately vested in their accrued benefits. The amounts contributed, plus earnings, would be overseen by an independent board of trustees administering the plan.

Advantages

- SCPs being proposed and considered across the country[10] could help millions of private sector workers without access to any pension plan.

Disadvantages

- Investment returns will remain subpar.
- SCPs are not portable for workers moving out of state.
- The plans are highly complex to administer for companies with employees in multiple states.
- In all Secure Choice models, workers can opt out of their individual accounts and are likely to do so if they need short-term funds for financial exigencies.
- No SCP models feature a presumed annuity payout or pooled investment options.
- 2017 Federal legislation essentially bars these plans.

AFSCME RETIREMENT PROGRAM

The State Supplemental Social Security Act proposed by the American Federation of State, County, and Municipal

Employees (AFSCME) is a mandated, advance-funded supplement to Social Security.

Under this plan, states raise payroll taxes to pay for benefits computed with Social Security actuarial methodology. Employees must have forty quarters of covered service to qualify for any benefit. If they move out of state, both employee and employer contributions are returned at age sixty-two.[11]

Advantages

- This ambitious proposal would eventually entail a federally mandated supplement to Social Security.
- It improves upon other proposals in filling the void from the erosion of defined-benefit plans.

Disadvantages

- The proposal received little support in state legislatures, which found tax-neutral Secure Choice proposals more popular.

AARP'S "WORK AND SAVE"

AARP's "Work and Save" proposal aims to support businesses in creating private retirement savings accounts for employees based on the 529 plan (or "qualified tuition plan") model. This retirement savings vehicle would be authorized by the state, run by the private sector, and professionally managed.

Work and Save has five core principles: financial freedom, voluntary participation, portability, saving taxpayer dollars, and no risk. It allows money saved by participants to travel with the owner. It provides tax advantages to enrollees and is available to everyone, including small businesses and low-income employees. And the cost is low to taxpayers and participants.

Advantages

- Work and Save has garnered support from a range of aging, human services, business, and labor groups across the country.
- More than a dozen states have considered legislation of this kind. Massachusetts, California, and Oregon have already enacted it.
- AARP surveys show support for Work and Save among a majority of workers who presently have no access to any retirement plan.

Disadvantages

- The program is voluntary, making it vulnerable to low participation and withdrawals.
- As with 401(k)s, investment returns will be substandard.
- Benefits cannot be annuitized.

WORKING LONGER

People facing inadequate retirement income often rely on working longer as a solution. Many of these individuals say they plan to "die at their desk." Unfortunately, as they age, they are also confronting an increasingly unfriendly job market. Employers often prefer to hire younger workers, leaving older ones to face longer periods of unemployment. The share of older workers with physically demanding jobs (including stooping and bending) is increasing, and the share of jobs reported as easy is falling. Poor health—either one's own or one's spouse's—can make work impossible. All things considered, older workers often end up being forced to retire earlier than planned.

According to an Employment Benefit Research Institute confidence survey, workers generally expect to retire at age sixty-five.[12] However, the average age of retirement is much lower, around age sixty-two.[13] If anything, the gap between expectation and reality seems to be widening. From 2010 to 2015, the number of retirees who stopped working earlier than expected rose by 9 percent due to poor health, layoffs, lack of training or retraining, or a failure to get promoted.[14] Once workers reach age fifty-five, they begin to experience a decline in earnings, regardless of education level.

In sum, the harsh realities of the labor market make it difficult or impossible to depend on employment until age seventy to maintain living standards into retirement. Work in old age is not the solution to the retirement crisis.

Advantages

- Older workers earn more income and continue working at jobs that interest them.

Disadvantages

- Working in old age may degrade the health of the worker.
- Those with full-time jobs cannot care for dependent family members.
- High rates of long-term unemployment and falling wages are prevalent among older workers.
- Older workers face age discrimination from employers.
- Investment and annuitization issues remain unaddressed.

APPENDIX C

LOOKING AT RETIREMENT COVERAGE
ACROSS THE COUNTRY

State	Workers with Retirement Coverage (%)
Alabama	39
Alaska	54
Arizona	43
Arkansas	43
California	44
Colorado	50
Connecticut	58
Delaware	58
District of Columbia	58
Florida	42
Georgia	45
Hawaii	59
Idaho	48
Illinois	51
Indiana	51
Iowa	59

(continued)

(Continued)

State	Workers with Retirement Coverage (%)
Kansas	57
Kentucky	45
Louisiana	48
Maine	51
Maryland	58
Massachusetts	55
Michigan	54
Minnesota	52
Mississippi	45
Missouri	60
Montana	55
Nebraska	53
Nevada	43
New Hampshire	56
New Jersey	47
New Mexico	40
New York	51
North Carolina	49
North Dakota	55
Ohio	54
Oklahoma	40
Oregon	48
Pennsylvania	55
Rhode Island	54
South Carolina	40
South Dakota	54

State	Workers with Retirement Coverage (%)
Tennessee	42
Texas	43
Utah	51
Vermont	51
Virginia	58
Washington	54
West Virginia	50
Wisconsin	58
Wyoming	55

Notes: Coverage rates are calculated as a three-year average. Sample includes all workers who reported working thirty-five hours per week or more.

Source: Author's calculation using the Annual Social and Economic Supplement (ASEC) to the Current Population Survey (CPS) for 2014–2016.

NOTES

1. SOCIETY'S RETIREMENT CRISIS

1. "The Retirement Gamble," *Frontline*, April 23, 2013, http://www
.pbs.org/wgbh/frontline/film/retirement-gamble/transcript/.
2. Society of Actuaries, The American Academy of Actuaries,
"Retirement Plan Preferences Survey: Report Of Findings," 2004,
https://www.soa.org/files/research/projects/PreferencesReport2
-5-FINAL-V2.pdf.
3. Social Security Administration, Annual Statistical Supplement,
2016: Table 6.B5.1, https://www.ssa.gov/policy/docs/statcomps
/supplement/2016/supplement16.pdf.
4. Samantha Costa, "Health Buzz: Americans Are Living Longer," *U.S. News & World Report*, January 21, 2016, http://health
.usnews.com/health-news/.
5. Aon Hewitt, "The 2012 Real Deal: 2012 Retirement Income
Adequacy at Large Companies: Highlights," 2012, http://www
.aon.com/attachments/human-capital-consulting/The_2012
_Real_Deal_Highlights.pdf.
6. Keith Miller, David Madland, and Christian E. Weller, "The
Reality of the Retirement Crisis," Center for American Progress,
January 26, 2015, https://www.americanprogress.org/issues
/economy/report/2015/01/26/105394/the-reality-of-the
-retirement-crisis.html.

7. A note about median and average annual earnings used throughout the book. The Bureau of Labor Statistics (BLS) reports median weekly earnings for full-time U.S. workers (thirty-five hours or more per week). In the first quarter of 2017, according to BLS, the median weekly wage for full-time workers was $855. (Bureau of Labor Statistics, Economic News Release, "Table 1. Median Usual Weekly Earnings of Full-Time Wage and Salary Workers by Sex, Quarterly Averages, Seasonally Adjusted," Accessed April 26, 2017, https://www.bls.gov/news.release /wkyeng.t01.htm.) Assuming full-time workers are paid for fifty weeks per year, the estimated median annual wage is more than $42,000; for fifty-two weeks, it is $44,460. (Social Security Administration, Office of the Chief Actuary, "Wage Statistics for 2015," April 26, 2015. Accessed April 26, 2017, https://www .ssa.gov/cgi-bin/netcomp.cgi?year=2015.)

8. Diane Oakley and Kelly Kenneally, "Retirement Security 2015: Roadmap for Policy Makers: Americans' Views of the Retirement Crisis," National Institute for Retirement Security, March 2015, http://www.nirsonline.org/index.php?option=content &task=view&id=881.html.

9. Teresa Ghilarducci and Zachary Knauss, "More Middle Class Workers Will Be Poor Retirees," Schwartz Center for Economic Policy Analysis and Department of Economics, The New School for Social Research, Policy Note Series, 2015, http://www .economicpolicyresearch.org/images/docs/retirement_security _background/Downward_Mobility.pdf.

10. Obama White House, "The Effects of Conflicted Investment Advice on Retirement Savings," February 2015, https://obama whitehouse.archives.gov/sites/default/files/docs/cea_coi _report_final.pdf.

11. "We'll Live to 100—How Can We Afford it?' (White Paper), World Economic Forum, May 2017, https://www.weforum.org /whitepapers/we-ll-live-to-100-how-can-we-afford-it.

12. The exceptions are workers with existing 401(k)s or defined-benefit plans, who may stay with them if they so choose.

2. HOW WE GOT HERE: AMERICA'S BROKEN RETIREMENT SYSTEM

1. Deirdre Fernandes, "A Warning on Realities of Work, Retirement," *Boston Globe*, November 30, 2014; Center for Retirement Research. "Data Fact Sheets: Pension Participation of All Workers, by Type of Plan, 1989–2013," http://crr.bc.edu/wp-content/uploads/1012/01/Pension-coverage1.pdf.
2. These defined-benefit plans were not a panacea. Employers could provide them—or dissolve them—at their discretion. Most smaller firms never offered them in the first place. Even when a pension was available, workers were required to stay at a job full time for at least five to ten years to vest for eligibility. And when workers changed employers, the pensions usually were not portable.
3. Center on Budget and Policy Priorities, "Policy Basics: Top Ten Facts About Social Security," August 13, 2015, http://www.cbpp.org/research/social-security/policy-basics-top-ten-facts-about-social-security.
4. Scott Tong, "Father of Modern 401(k) Says It Fails Many Americans," Marketplace.org, June 13, 2013, http://www.marketplace.org/2013/06/13/sustainability/consumed/father-modern-401k-says-it-fails-many-americans.html.
5. Tom Anderson, "The Surprising Origins of Your 401(k)," Nasdaq.com, July 8, 2013, http://www.nasdaq.com/article/the-surprising-origins-of-your-401k-cm258685.
6. Tong, "Father of Modern 401(k) Says It Fails Many Americans."
7. Kelley Holland, "For Millions, 401(k) Plans Have Fallen Short," CNBC.com, March 23, 2015, http://www.cnbc.com/2015/03/20/l-it-the-401k-is-a-failure.html.

8. Patty Kujawa, "A 'Father's' Wisdom: An Interview with Ted Benna," Workforce.com, January 20, 2012, http://www.work force.com/2012/01/20/a-fathers-wisdom-an-interview-with -ted-benna/.

9. Statistics are based on the author's calculations using the March Supplement to the Current Population Survey. See Appendix D for a complete list of coverage rages by state.

10. U.S. Government Accountability Office, "Retirement Security: Low Defined Contribution Savings May Pose Challenges," GAO-16-408, May 5, 2016, https://www.gao.gov/products /GAO-16-408.

11. Christopher Flavelle, "The Inequality of Retirement Anxiety," BloombergView, February 18, 2015, https://www.bloomberg.com /view/articles/2015-02-18/the-inequality-of-retirement-anxiety.

12. Quoted in Elizabeth Olson, "For Many Women, Adequate Pensions Are Still a Far Reach." *New York Times*, June 3, 2016, http://www.nytimes.com/2016/.

3. SIX KEY PROBLEMS

1. U.S. Government Accountability Office, "Retirement Security: Most Households Approaching Retirement Have Low Savings," Report to the Ranking Member, Subcommittee on Primary Health and Retirement Security, Committee on Health, Education, Labor, and Pensions, U.S. Senate, May 2015, http://www .gao.gov/assets/680/670153.pdf.

2. National Association of State Retirement Administrators, "NASRA Issue Brief: Public Pension Plan Investment Return Assumptions," 2015, updated February 2017, http://www.nasra .org/files/Issue%20Briefs/NASRAInvReturnAssumptBrief.pdf.

3. As quoted in Nick Summers, "In Australia, Retirement Savings Done Right," Bloomberg.com, May 30, 2013, http://www .bloomberg.com/news/articles/2013-05-30/in-australia -retirement-saving-done-right.

4. Allison Schrager, "Behind the Venture Capital Boom: Public Pensions," Bloomberg.com, September 23, 2014, http://www .bloomberg.com/news/articles/2014-09-23/are-public -pensions-inflating-a-venture-capital-bubble.

5. Teresa Ghilarducci and Zachary Knauss, "More Middle Class Workers Will Be Poor Retirees," Schwartz Center for Economic Policy Analysis and Department of Economics, New School for Social Research, Policy Note Series, 2015, http://www.economic policyresearch.org/images/docs/retirement_security_back ground/Downward_Mobility.pdf.

6. U.S. Government Accountability Office, "Retirement Security: Low Defined Contribution Savings May Pose Challenges," GAO-16 -408, May 5, 2016, https://www.gao.gov/products /GAO-16-408.

7. For individuals born in 1960 and thereafter, Social Security pays full benefits at age sixty-seven and a bonus up until age seventy. Most people, however, do not wait until their full retirement age to start collecting. In 2013, the latest data available, 42 percent of men and 48 percent of women collected Social Security at age sixty-two—an indication of reduced labor force activity, if not full retirement.

8. Ritholtz, Barry, "Tackling the Nastiest, Hardest Problem in Finance," *Bloomberg View*, June 5, 2017.

4. RESCUING RETIREMENT: A FOUR-PRONGED SOLUTION

1. Franklin D. Roosevelt, "Public Papers of the President of the United States," Vol. 9. Washington, D.C.: Office of the Federal Register, National Archives and Records Administration, 1940.

2. There is no precisely accurate measure, and the median wage changes each year, so for simplicity's sake we have chosen to use $40,000, the minimum salary that generates the full $600 GRA tax credit.

3. This is based on 2017 federal tax rates.

4. The Saver's Credit is a nonrefundable tax break of up to $2,000 per year. It is available to low- or moderate-income taxpayers who make voluntary, salary-deferral contributions to their employer-sponsored 401(k), 403(b), SIMPLE, SEP, or government 457 plan, or to traditional IRAs and Roth IRAs.

5. Pew Charitable Trusts, "Small Business Views on Retirement Saving Plans." 2017, http://www.pewtrusts.org/en/research-and -analysis/issue-briefs/2017/01/small-business-views-on -retirement-savings-plans

6. Aon Hewitt, "Customize DC Investments for Participant Success," July 2015, http://www.aon.com/attachments/human -capital-consulting/custom-dc-investments-for-participant -success-wp-july2015.pdf.

7. Although overall GRA fees will be lower, the GRA board will charge approximately 20 to 30 basis points per year; the higher the balance, the lower the fee.

8. The typical 401(k) fees (outsourced chief investment officer [OCIO] fees) are taken from a 2016 Cerulli OCIO survey. For assets of more than $1 billion, fees are 10 basis points. They slide upward toward 30 basis points as the asset pool size drops to $100 million. Defined-contribution plan/401(k) OCIO fees for funds ranging from $1 billion to $100 million are between 5 and 20 basis points.

9. Aon Hewett, 2015.

10. National Association of State Retirement Administrators, "NASRA Issue Brief: Public Pension Plan Investment Return Assumptions," 2015, updated February 2017, http://www.nasra .org/files/Issue%20Briefs/NASRAInvReturnAssumptBrief.pdf.

5. CASE STUDIES

1. Richard Eisenberg, "To Solve the U.S. Retirement Crisis, Look to Australia," *Forbes,* August 19, 2013, http://www.forbes.com /sites/nextavenue/2013/08/19/to-solve-the-u-s-retirement -crisis-look-to-australia/#d03acaf445f6.

2. Nick Summers, "In Australia, Retirement Savings Done Right," Bloomberg.com, May 30, 2013, http://www.bloomberg.com /news/articles/2013-05-30/in-australia-retirement-saving-done -right.

3. Eisenberg, "To Solve the U.S. Retirement Crisis, Look to Australia."

4. Bill Shorten, "20 Years of Superannuation," Address to ASFA Superannuation Guarantee Dinner, Australian Treasury Portfolio Ministers, August 16, 2011, http://ministers.treasury.gov. au/DisplayDocs.aspx?doc=speeches/2011/028.htm&pageID= 005&min=brsa&Year=&DocType=1.

5. Trish Power, "Liberals Slow Down SG Increase Until July 2025," SuperGuide, January 12, 2016, https://www.superguide.com.au /boost-your-superannuation/liberals-sg-lisc.

6. Tim Stewart, "Super Satisfaction Increasing: Roy Morgan," *Investor Daily*, May 28, 2015, http://www.investordaily.com.au /superannuation/.

7. Association of Superannuation Funds of Australia, "Superannuation Statistics," 2015, https://www.superannuation.asn.au /resources/superannuation-statistics.

8. Alicia Munnell, Anthony Webb, and Francesca Golub-Sass, "The National Retirement Risk Index: An Update," Center for Retirement Research at Boston College, October 2012, http://crr .bc.edu/briefs/the-national-retirement-risk-index-an-update/.

9. Australian Centre for Financial Studies. "Melbourne Mercer Global Pension Index," 2015, http://www. globalpensionindex .com/wp-content/uploads/Melbourne-Mercer-Global-Pension -Index-2015-Report-Web.pdf.

10. Ibid.

11. James F. Peltz, "Obama Wants to Help California Create More Retirement-Savings Accounts." *Los Angeles Times*, July 13, 2015. http://www.latimes.com/business/.

12. Letter to the Department of Labor by the National Association of Insurance and Financial Advisors, January 2016.

13. Mark Miller, "Can State Auto-IRA Plans Improve Retirement Security?" Retirement Revised, October 24, 2015, http://retirement revised.com/can-state-auto-ira-plans-improve-retirement-security/.

14. Tara Siegel Bernard, "More States Are Initiating Programs to Encourage Retirement Savings," *New York Times*, November 16, 2015, http://www.nytimes.com/2015/.

6. WHY NOT JUST EXPAND SOCIAL SECURITY?

1. Gallup Poll, "Social Security," 2017.

2. Pew Research Center, "Political Polarization in the American Public," June 12, 2014, http://www.people-press.org/2014/06/12/political-polarization-in-the-american-public/.

3. Among the proposed reforms are eliminating the cap on FICA taxes, lifting the FICA tax rate to 7.2 percent, raising the minimum Social Security benefit, and increasing cost-of-living adjustments. Jasmine V. Tucker, Virginia P. Reno, and Thomas N. Bethel, "Strengthening Social Security: What Do Americans Want?" National Academy of Social Insurance, January 2013, https://www.nasi.org/research/2013/report-strengthening-social-security-what-do-americans-want.

7. GROWING SUPPORT FROM THE AMERICAN PEOPLE AND A MANDATE FOR CONGRESS

1. Diane Oakley and Kelly Kenneally, "Retirement Security 2017: A Roadmap for Policy Makers," National Institute on Retirement Security, February 2017, http://www.nirsonline.org/storage/nirs/documents/2017%20Conference/2017_opinion_nirs_final_web.pdf.

QUESTIONS AND ANSWERS ON THE GUARANTEED
RETIREMENT ACCOUNT

1. Keith Blackwell and Teresa Ghilarducci, "The Guarantee's Cost to the Government: SCEPA Policy Brief," Schwartz Center for Economic Policy Analysis, The New School for Social Research, 2016.

APPENDIX A: THE COST OF A PRINCIPAL
PROTECTION GUARANTEE

We acknowledge Keith Blackwell, economics graduate student at the New School for Social Research, for his invaluable help in writing this appendix.

1. For model specification, we used historical pension fund returns from 1945 to 2015 to fit two distributions: Gaussian and a non-central t-distribution. In all models, we combine historical fits with expectations of future returns.
2. William G. Gale, David C. John, and Bryan Kim, "You Get What You Pay For: Guaranteed Returns in Retirement Saving Accounts," Policy Brief, Economic Studies at Brookings, March 2016, www.brookings.edu/research/you-get-what-you-pay-for-guaranteed-returns-in-retirement-saving-accounts/.
3. Alicia H. Munnell, Alex Golub-Sass, Richard W. Kopcke, and Anthony Webb, "What Does It Cost to Guarantee Returns?" Center for Retirement Research at Boston College, February 2009, No. 9-4, http://crr.bc.edu/wp-content/uploads/2009/02/IB_9-4.pdf.
4. David M. Stubbs and Nari Rhee, "Can a Publicly Sponsored Retirement Plan for Private Sector Workers Guarantee Benefits at No Risk to the State?" Policy Brief, University of California, Berkeley Center for Labor Research and Education, August 2012, http://laborcenter.berkeley.edu/pdf/2012/ca_guaranteed_retirement_study12.pdf.

5. Olivia S. Mitchell, "The Irresponsibility of States Guaranteeing Pension Returns," The Experts Blog. *Wall Street Journal*, November 5, 2015, http://blogs.wsj.com/experts/.
6. Marie-Eve Lachance and Olivia S. Mitchell, "Understanding Individual Account Guarantees," Working Paper 9195, National Bureau of Economic Research, September 2002, http://www.nber.org/papers/w9195.pdf.

APPENDIX B: GRAs VERSUS OTHER POLICY SOLUTIONS

1. This is an excerpt from an article first published by The New School SCEPA. Teresa Ghilarducci, Bridget Fisher, and Zachary Knauss, "Now Is the Time to Add Retirement Accounts to Social Security: The Guaranteed Retirement Account Proposal," The New School SCEPA, June 2015, www.economicpolicyresearch.org/images/docs/retirement_security... /GRA_3.0.pdf.
2. Pew Charitable Trusts, "President Obama's Budget Includes Automatic IRA Proposal and Expansion of Saver's Credit for 401(k)/IRA Savings" (Press release), July 21, 2014, http://www.pewtrusts.org/en/about/newsroom/press-releases /0001/01/01/president-obamas-budget-includes-automatic-ira -proposal-and-expansion-of-savers-credit-for-401k-ira-savings.
3. Emily Brandon, "New Details of Obama's Automatic IRA Proposal," *U.S. News & World Report*, February 2, 2010, http:// money.usnews.com/money/.
4. Executive Office of the President, Office of Management and Budget. *A New Era of Responsibility: Renewing America's Promise* (Washington, D.C.: U.S. Government Printing Office, 2009).
5. Aon Corporation, "Automatic IRA Legislation," September 2010, http://www.aon.com/attachments/auto_ira_sep2010.pdf.
6. U.S. Department of the Treasury, "About myRA," last updated October 18, 2016, https://myra.gov/about/.

7. Alicia H. Munnell, "The myRA Addresses a Serious Problem," *Marketwatch*, February 12, 2014, http://blogs.marketwatch.com /encore/2014/02/12/the-myra-addresses-a-serious-problem/.

8. Ben Steverman, "There's Something about MyRA," Bloomberg. com, January 2014, www.bloomberg.com/news.

9. Joel Kranc, "Institutional Investor: States Move to Implement Retirement Accounts," Schwartz Center for Economic and Policy Analysis, The New School, February 11, 2015, http://www .economicpolicyresearch.org/index.php/wealth-insecurity -news/1518-institutional-investor-states-move-to-implement -retirement-accounts.

10. More information on the progress of state GRAs is available at http://www.ncpers.org/files/2014_02_20%20NCPERS%20 MD%20Testimony_FINAL%20(1) pdf; http://www.usretire-mentfacts.com/state-activity-2/; and http://www.seiu1000.org /sites/main/files/fileattachments/040814_update.pdf.

11. Contributions are returned with 5 percent compounded interest or actual returns from the initial contribution date, whichever is lower.

12. Employee Benefit Research Institute, "2015 RCS Fact Sheet #2: Expectations about Retirement," April 2015, https://www.ebri .org/surveys/rcs/2015/.

13. Gary Burtless, "Can Educational Attainment Explain the Rise in Labor Force Participation at Older Ages?" Center for Retirement Research at Boston College, Brief 13-13, September 2013, http:// crr.bc.edu/briefs/can-educational-attainment-explain-the-rise-in -labor-force-participation-at-older-ages/; Henry Aaron and Gary Burtless, *Closing the Deficit: How Much Can Later Retirement Help?* (Washington, D.C.: Brookings Institution Press, 2013).

14. Ruth Helman, Craig Copeland, and Jack VanDerhei, "The 2015 Retirement Confidence Survey: Having a Retirement Savings Plan a Key Factor in Americans' Retirement Confidence," Employee Benefit Research Institute, Issue Brief 413, April 2015, https://www.ebri.org/pdf/briefspdf/EBRI_IB_413_Apr15 _RCS-2015.pdf.

BIBLIOGRAPHY

Aaron, Henry, and Gary Burtless. *Closing the Deficit: How Much Can Later Retirement Help?* (Washington, D.C.: Brookings Institution Press, 2013).

Anderson, Tom. "The Surprising Origins of Your 401(k)." Nasdaq .com, July 8, 2013. http://www.nasdaq.com/article/the-surprising -origins-of-your-401k-cm258685.

Aon Hewitt. "Automatic IRA Legislation." Aon.com, September 2010. http://www.aon.com/attachments/auto_ira_sep2010.pdf.

——. "Customize DC Investments for Participant Success." Aon .com, July 2015. http://www.aon.com/attachments/human-capital -consulting/custom-dc-investments-for-participant-success-wp -july2015.pdf.

——. "The 2012 Real Deal: 2012 Retirement Income Adequacy at Large Companies: Highlights." Aon.com, 2012. http://www.aon .com/attachments/human-capital-consulting/The_2012_Real _Deal_Highlights.pdf.

Arias, Daniele, and Teresa Ghilarducci. "Employers Stake in Pension Reform." SCEPA Working Paper 2011-3. Schwartz Center for Economic Policy Analysis, The New School for Social Research, February 2011. http://www.economicpolicyresearch.org/images /docs/SCEPA_blog/guaranteeing_retirement_income/Ghilarducci _WP_2011_3.pdf.

Association of Superannuation Funds of Australia. "Superannuation Statistics." 2015. https://www.superannuation.asn.au/resources /superannuation-statistics.

Australian Centre for Financial Studies. "Melbourne Mercer Global Pension Index," 2015. http://www. globalpensionindex.com/wp -content/uploads/Melbourne-Mercer-Global-Pension-Index -2015-Report-Web.pdf.

Bender, Keith, and Natalia Jivan. "What Makes Retirees Happy?" Issue in Brief 28. Center for Retirement Research at Boston College, February 2005. http://crr.bc.edu/wp-content/uploads/2005/02 /ib_28.pdf.

Blackwell, Keith, and Teresa Ghilarducci. "The Guarantee's Cost to the Government." The New School SCEPA Policy Brief. Schwartz Center for Economic Policy Analysis, 2016. http://www.economic policyresearch.org/images/docs/retirement_security_background /GRA_3.0.pdf.

Board of Governors of the Federal Reserve System. "Report on the Economic Well-Being of U.S. Households in 2014." May 2015. https:// www.federalreserve.gov/econresdata/2014-report-economic -well-being-us-households-201505.pdf.

Bonen, Anthony. "Older Workers and Employers' Demands." Policy Note. Schwartz Center for Economic Policy Analysis, January 2013. https://docs.google.com/file/d/0B35b9afh6ZgZZEFwb TI4V3JsM1U/edit.

Brandon, Emily. "New Details of Obama's Automatic IRA Proposal." U.S. News & World Report, February 2, 2010. http://money.usnews .com/money/.

Burtless, Gary. "Can Educational Attainment Explain the Rise in Labor Force Participation at Older Ages?" Brief 13-13. Center for Retirement Research at Boston College, September 2013. http:// crr.bc.edu/briefs/can-educational-attainment-explain-the-rise-in -labor-force-participation-at-older-ages/.

Center on Budget and Policy Priorities. "Policy Basics: Top Ten Facts About Social Security." August 13, 2015. http://www.cbpp.org

/research/social-security/policy-basics-top-ten-facts-about
-social-security.

Center for Retirement Research. "Data Fact Sheets: Pension Participation of All Workers, by Type of Plan, 1989–2013." http://crr
.bc.edu/wp-content/uploads/1012/01/Pension-coverage1.pdf.

Cerulli Associates. "U.S. Advisor Metrics 2016: Combatting Fee and
Margin Pressure." https://www.cerulli.com/publications/us-advisor
-metrics-2016-combatting-fee-and-margin-pressure-P0003ER.

Costa, Samantha. "Health Buzz: Americans Are Living Longer." *U.S.
News & World Report*, January 21, 2016. http://health.usnews
.com/health-news/.

Crowley, Joseph. "Vice Chair Crowley Unveils New, Groundbreaking
Plan to Address Savings Crisis in U.S. and Help American Families
Save." Keynote at Center for American Progress Action Fund Event,
2015.http://crowley.house.gov/press-release/vice-chair-crowley-unveils
-new-groundbreaking-plan-address-savings-crisis-us-and-help.

Eisenberg, Richard. "To Solve the U.S. Retirement Crisis, Look to
Australia." *Forbes*, August 19, 2013. http://www.forbes.com/sites
/nextavenue/2013/08/19/to-solve-the-u-s-retirement-crisis-look
-to-australia/#d03acaf445f6.

Employee Benefit Research Institute. "FAQs About Benefits—
Retirement Issues." accessed May 20, 2016. https://www.ebri.org
/publications/benfaq/index.cfm?fa=retfaq14.

——. "2015 RCS Fact Sheet #2: Expectations About Retirement."
Retirement Confidence Survey, April 2015. https://www.ebri.org
/surveys/rcs/2015/.

Executive Office of the President, Office of Management and Budget.
A New Era of Responsibility: Renewing America's Promise (Washington, D.C.: U.S. Government Printing Office, 2009).

Fernandes, Deirdre. "A Warning on Realities of Work, Retirement."
Boston Globe, November 30, 2014.

Flavelle, Christopher. "The Inequality of Retirement Anxiety." *Bloomberg View*, February 18, 2015. https://www.bloomberg.com/view
/articles/2015-02-18/the-inequality-of-retirement-anxiety.

Gale, William G., David C. John, and Bryan Kim. "You Get What You Pay For: Guaranteed Returns in Retirement Saving Accounts." Policy Brief. Economic Studies at Brookings, March 2016. www.brookings.edu/research/you-get-what-you-pay-for-guaranteed-returns-in-retirement-saving-accounts/.

Gallup Poll. Social Security. 2017. Accessed July 12, 2017. http://www.gallup.com/poll/1693/social-security.aspx.

Government Accounting Office (GAO). "Individual Retirement Accounts: IRS Could Bolster Enforcement on Multimillion Dollar Accounts, but More Direction from Congress Is Needed." Washington, D.C.. GAO-15-16: Published: Oct 20, 2014. Publicly Released: Nov 19, 2014

Ghilarducci, Teresa, Bridget Fisher, and Zachary Knauss. "Now Is the Time to Add Retirement Accounts to Social Security: The Guaranteed Retirement Account Proposal." The New School SCEPA, June 2015. www.economicpolicyresearch.org/images/docs/retirement_security.../GRA_3.0.pdf.

Ghilarducci, Teresa, Bridget Fisher, Kyle Moore, and Anthony Webb. "Gender and Racial Disparities in Physical Job Demands of Older Workers." Policy Note. Schwartz Center for Economic Policy Analysis, The New School for Social Research, October 2016. http://www.economicpolicyresearch.org/images/docs/research/retirement_security/2016-4_Gender_Racial_Gaps_in_Older_Workers_Physical_Job_Demands.pdf.

Ghilarducci, Teresa, Bridget Fisher, Siavash Radpour, and Anthony Webb. "401(k) Plans: A Failed Experiment." Policy Note. Schwartz Center for Economic Policy Analysis, The New School for Social Research, 2016. http://www.economicpolicyresearch.org/images/docs/research/retirement_security/401k_Plans_A_Failed_Experiment.pdf.

Ghilarducci, Teresa, and Hamilton E. James. "A Smarter Plan to Make Retirement Savings Last." *New York Times*, January 1, 2016. http://www.nytimes.com/2016/.

Ghilarducci, Teresa, and Zachary Knauss. "More Middle Class Workers Will Be Poor Retirees." Policy Note. Schwartz Center for Economic Policy Analysis and Department of Economics, The New School, 2015. http://www.economicpolicyresearch.org /images/docs/retirement_security_background/Downward _Mobility.pdf.

Ghilarducci, Teresa, Joelle Saad-Lessler, and Kate Bahn. "Are U.S. Workers Ready for Retirement? Trends in Plan Sponsorship, Participation, and Preparedness." *Journal of Pension Benefits* (Winter 2015): 25–39.

Helman, Ruth, Craig Copeland, and Jack VanDerhei. "The 2015 Retirement Confidence Survey: Having a Retirement Savings Plan a Key Factor in Americans' Retirement Confidence." Issue Brief 413. Employee Benefit Research Institute, April 2015. https:// www.ebri.org/pdf/briefspdf/EBRI_IB_413_Apr15_RCS-2015 .pdf.

Holland, Kelley. "For Millions, 401(k) Plans Have Fallen Short." CNBC.com, March 23, 2015. http://www.cnbc.com/2015/03/20 /l-it-the-401k-is-a-failure.html.

Joint Committee on Taxation. "Estimates of Federal Tax Expenditures for Fiscal Years 2016-2020." January 17, 2017. https:// www.jct.gov/publications.html?func=startdown&id=4971 %20page%2038.

Johnson, Richard, Gordon Mermin, and Matthew Resseger. "Employment at Older Ages and the Changing Nature of Work." Urban Policy Institute, 2008. http://www.urban.org/research /publication/employment-older-ages-and-changing-nature -work.

Kujawa, Patty. "A 'Father's' Wisdom: An Interview with Ted Benna." Workforce.com, January 20, 2012. http://www.workforce.com /2012/01/20/a-fathers-wisdom-an-interview-with-ted-benna/.

Kranc, Joel. "Institutional Investor: States Move to Implement Retirement Accounts." Schwartz Center for Economic and Policy

Analysis, The New School, February 11, 2015. http://www.economic policyresearch.org/index.php/wealth-insecurity-news/1518 -institutional-investor-states-move-to-implement-retirement -accounts.

Lachance, Marie-Eve, and Olivia S. Mitchell. "Understanding Individual Account Guarantees." Working Paper 9195. National Bureau of Economic Research, September 2002. http://www.nber.org /papers/w9195.pdf.

Lieber, Ron. "Getting a Reverse Mortgage, but Not from a Celebrity." *New York Times*, June 10, 2016. http://www.nytimes .com/2016/.

MSCI Analytics. "InvestorForce Report."MSCI.com. https://www .msci.com/documents/1296102/1636401/InvestorForce_Report .pdf/1b6f2b80-dbfe-4f69-995a-4e2131fbc2fa.

Miller, Keith., David Madland, and Christian E. Weller. "The Reality of the Retirement Crisis." Center for American Progress, January 26, 2015. https://www.americanprogress.org/issues/economy /report/2015/01/26/105394/the-reality-of-the-retirement-crisis .html.

Miller, Mark. "Can State Auto-IRA Plans Improve Retirement Security?" Retirement Revised, October 24, 2015. http://retirement revised.com/can-state-auto-ira-plans-improve-retirement -security/.

Mitchell, Olivia S. "The Irresponsibility of States Guaranteeing Pension Returns." The Experts Blog. *Wall Street Journal*, November 5, 2015. http://blogs.wsj.com/experts/.

Munnell, Alicia H. "The myRA Addresses a Serious Problem." Marketwatch, February 12, 2014. http://blogs.marketwatch.com /encore/2014/02/12/the-myra-addresses-a-serious-problem/.

Munnell, Alicia H., Jean-Pierre Aubry, and Caroline V. Crawford. "Investment Returns: Defined Benefit Vs. Defined Contribution Plans." Center for Retirement Research at Boston College. December 2015, no. 15-21. http://crr.bc.edu/wp-content/uploads/2015/12 /IB_15-21.pdf.

Munnell, Alicia H., Alex Golub-Sass, Richard W. Kopcke, and Anthony Webb. "What Does It Cost to Guarantee Returns?" Center for Retirement Research at Boston College, February 2009, no. 9-4. http://crr.bc.edu/wp-content/uploads/2009/02 /IB_9-4.pdf.

Munnell, Alicia H., Mauricio Soto, and Alex Golub-Sass. "Are Older Men Healthy Enough to Work?" Center for Retirement Research at Boston College. October 2008, no. 8-17. http:// citeseerx.ist.psu.edu/viewdoc/download;jsessionid=6AF1E978 B3986B4B74776E3E8D7DE4FD?doi=10.1.1.620.4393&rep=r ep1&type=pdf.

Munnell, Alicia H., Anthony Webb, and Francesca Golub-Sass. "The National Retirement Risk Index: An Update." Center for Retirement Research at Boston College, October 2012. http:// crr.bc.edu/briefs/the-national-retirement-risk-index-an -update/.

National Association of State Retirement Administrators. "NASRA Issue Brief: Public Pension Plan Investment Return Assumptions." 2015, updated February 2017. http://www.nasra.org/files /Issue%20Briefs/NASRAInvReturnAssumptBrief.pdf.

National Association of Insurance and Financial Advisors. Letter objecting to DOL rule, January 19, 2016. https://www.dol.gov/sites /default/files/ebsa/laws-and-regulations/rules-and-regulations /public-comments/1210-AB71/00035.pdf.

National Institute on Aging. "Growing Older in America: The Health and Retirement Study." U.S. Department of Health and Human Services, 2007. https://d2cauhfh6h4x0p.cloudfront.net/s3fs-public /health_and_retirement_study_0.pdf.

Nyce, Steve, and Billie Jean Quade. "Annuities and Retirement Happiness." Willis Towers Watson, 2012. https://www.towerswatson .com/en/insights/newsletters/americas/insider/2012/annuities -and-retirement-happiness.

Oakley, Diane, and Kelly Kenneally. "Retirement Security 2015: Roadmap for Policy Makers: Americans' Views of the Retirement

Crisis." National Institute for Retirement Security, March 2015. http://www.nirsonline.org/index.php?option=content&task =view&id=881.html.

Obama White House. The Effects of Conflicted Investment Advice On Retirement Savings. February 2015. Accessed July 11 https:// obamawhitehouse.archives.gov/sites/default/files/docs/cea_coi _report_final.pdf.

"Retirement Security 2017: A Roadmap for Policy Makers." National Institute on Retirement Security, February 2017. http://www .nirsonline.org/storage/nirs/documents/2017%20Conference /2017_opinion_nirs_final_web.pdf.

Olson, Elizabeth. "For Many Women, Adequate Pensions Are Still a Far Reach." *New York Times*, June 3, 2016. http://www.nytimes .com/2016/.

Olshan, Jeremy. "'Father' of the 401(k)s Tough Love." Market-watch, November 22, 2011. http://blogs.marketwatch.com/encore /2011/11/22/father-of-the-401ks-tough-love/.

Panis, Constantijn. "Annuities and Retirement Satisfaction." Labor and Population Program, Working Paper 03-17. RAND, April 2003. https://www.rand.org/content/dam/rand/pubs/drafts/2008 /DRU3021.pdf.

Peltz, James F. "Obama Wants to Help California Create More Retire-ment-Savings Accounts." *Los Angeles Times*, July 13, 2015. http:// www.latimes.com/business/la-fi-0713-obama-retirement-savings -20150713-story.html.

Pew Charitable Trusts. "President Obama's Budget Includes Auto-matic IRA Proposal and Expansion of Saver's Credit for 401(k)/ IRA Savings." Press Release, July 21, 2014. http://www.pewtrusts .org/en/about/newsroom/press-releases/0001/01/01/president -obamas-budget-includes-automatic-ira-proposal-and-expansion -of-savers-credit-for-401k-ira-savings.

Pew Charitable trusts, "Small Business Views on Retirement Savings Plans." 2017. http://www.pewtrusts.org/en/research-and-analysis/issue -briefs/2017/01/small-business-views-on-retirement-savings-plans

Pew Research Center. "Political Polarization in the American Public." June 12, 2014. http://www.people-press.org/2014/06/12/political -polarization-in-the-american-public/.

Power, Trish. "Liberals Slow Down SG Increase Until July 2025." SuperGuide, January 12, 2016. https://www.superguide.com.au /boost-your-superannuation/liberals-sg-lisc.

Pramuk, Jacob. "New York Fed: Household Debt at Highest Level Since 2010." CNBC.com, November 19, 2015. http://www. CNBC .com/2015/11/19/new-york-fed-household-debt-at-highest-level -since-2010.html.

Rajnes, David. "An Evolving Pension System: Trends in Defined Benefit and Defined Contribution Plans." Issue Brief 249. Employee Benefit Research Institute, September 2002. https://papers.ssrn.com /sol3/papers.cfm?abstract_id=341100&rec=1&srcabs=907291&alg =1&pos=1.

"The Retirement Gamble." *Frontline*, April 23, 2013. http://www.pbs .org/wgbh/frontline/film/retirement-gamble/transcript/.

Rhee, Nari and Voivie, Ilana, The Continuing Retirement Savings Crisis (March 18, 2015). https://ssrn.com/abstract=2785723 or http://dx.doi.org/10.2139/ssrn.2785723.

Roosevelt, Franklin D. *Public Papers of the President of the United States*, vol. 9 (Washington, D.C.: Office of the Federal Register, National Archives and Records Administration, 1940).

Rutledge, Matthew S., April Yanyuan Wu, and Francis M. Vitagliano. "Do Tax Incentives Increase 401(k) Retirement Savings? Evidence From the Adoption of Catch-Up Contributions." Center for Retirement Research at Boston College, November 2014. http:// crr.bc.edu/working-papers/do-tax-incentives-increase-401k -retirement-saving-evidence-from-the-adoption-of-catch-up -contributions/.

Schrager, Allison. "Behind the Venture Capital Boom: Public Pensions." Bloomberg.com, September 23, 2014. http://www.bloomberg.com /news/articles/2014-09-23/are-public-pensions-inflating-a -venture-capital-bubble.

Shorten, Bill. "20 Years of Superannuation." Address to ASFA Superannuation Guarantee Dinner. Australian Treasury Portfolio Ministers, August 16, 2011. http://ministers.treasury.gov.au /DisplayDocs.aspx?doc=speeches/2011/028.htm&pageID =005&min=brsa&Year=&DocType=1.

Siegel Bernard, Tara. "More States Are Initiating Programs to Encourage Retirement Savings." *New York Times*, November 16, 2015. http://www.nytimes.com/2015/.

Social Security Online. "Wage Statistics for 2015." Office of the Chief Actuary, June 15, 2017. https://www.ssa.gov/cgi-bin/netcomp .cgi?year=2015.

Steurle, C. Eugene, and Caleb Quakenbush. "Social Security and Medicare Taxes and Benefits Over a Lifetime: An Update," The Urban Institute, 2012. http://www.urban.org/sites/default/files /publication/25831/412660-Social-Security-and-Medicare -Taxes-and-Benefits-Over-a-Lifetime—Update.PDF.

Steverman, Ben. "Small Companies Have a Big Retirement Problem," Bloomberg.com, January 2017. www.bloomberg.com/news/articles /2017-01-11/small-companies-have-a-big-retirement-problem.

——. "There's Something About MyRA." Bloomberg.com, January 2014. www.bloomberg.com/news.

Stewart, Tim. "Super Satisfaction Increasing: Roy Morgan." *Investor Daily*, May 28, 2015. http://www.investordaily.com.au/super annuation/.

Stubbs, David M., and Nari Rhee. "Can a Publicly Sponsored Retirement Plan for Private Sector Workers Guarantee Benefits at No Risk to the State?" Policy Brief. University of California, Berkeley Center for Labor Research and Education, August 2012. http:// laborcenter.berkeley.edu/pdf/2012/ca_guaranteed_retirement _study12.pdf.

Summers, Nick. "In Australia, Retirement Savings Done Right." Bloomberg.com, May 30, 2013. http://www.bloomberg.com/news /articles/2013-05-30/in-australia-retirement-saving-done-right.

Tergesen, Anne. "12 Things You Should Know About the myRA." Marketwatch, 2015. http://blogs.marketwatch.com/encore/2014/02/04/12-things-savers-should-know-about-the-myra/.

Tong, Scott. "Father of Modern 401(k) Says It Fails Many Americans." Marketplace.org, June 13, 2013. http://www. marketplace.org/2013/06/13/sustainability/consumed/father-modern-401k-says-it-fails-many-americans.html.

Tucker, Jasmine V., Virginia P. Reno, and Thomas N. Bethel. "Strengthening Social Security: What Do Americans Want?" National Academy of Social Insurance, January 2013. https://www.nasi.org/research/2013/report-strengthening-social-security-what-do-americans-want.

U.S. Department of the Treasury, "About myRA," last updated October 18, 2016. https://myra.gov/about/.

U.S. Government Accountability Office, "Retirement Security: Low Defined Contribution Savings May Pose Challenges." GAO-16-408. May 5, 2016. https://www.gao.gov/products/GAO-16-408.

"Retirement Security: Most Households Approaching Retirement Have Low Savings." Report to the Ranking Member, Subcommittee on Primary Health and Retirement Security, Committee on Health, Education, Labor, and Pensions, U.S. Senate, May 2015. http://www.gao.gov/assets/680/670153.pdf.

VanDerhei, Jack. "What Causes EBRI Retirement Readiness Ratings to Vary: Results from the 2014 Retirement Security Projection Model." Issue Brief 396. Employee Benefit Research Institute. February 2014. http://www.ebri.org/pdf/briefspdf/EBRI_IB_396_Feb14.RRRs2.pdf.

"Retirement Income Adequacy: Alternative Thresholds and the Importance of Future Eligibility in Defined Contribution Retirement Plans." Employee Benefit Research Institute. *Notes* 32, 4 (April 2011): 2–20. http://www.ebri.org/pdf/notespdf/EBRI_Notes_04_Apr-11.PolFor-RSPM.pdf.

Vasilogambros, Matt. "Americans Want to Save More Money. They Just Can't." *The Atlantic*, April 21, 2014. http://www.theatlantic .com/business/archive/2014/04/americans-want-to-save-more -money-they-just-cant/425376/.

Weiland, Noah. "Senate Narrowly Passes Rollback of Obama-Era 'Auto-IRA' Rule." *New York Times*, March 30, 2017. https://www .nytimes.com/2017/03/30/business/labor-department-retirement -savings-account.html?_r=0.

Weltman, Barbara. "Weighing the Pros and Cons of Obama's myRA." Inc.com, 2015. https://www.inc.com/barbara-weltman/weighing -pros-and-cons-of-obamas-myra.html?cid=search.

INDEX

capital gains, 62
case studies, 83–87
Center for Retirement Research, 33–34, *38*
challenges: of annuities, *73*; of 401(k)'s, 72; for policy makers, 13; of retirement system, 1; of savings, 6, 29; to workers, 2
child care, 3
Congress, U.S., 123
Congressional Budget Office, 71, 120
contributions: from employers, 52–53, 57–59; to GRA, *45*, 55–56, 78; mandates on, 52, 106; to savings, 18, *49–52*; from workers, 11–12, 52–56
cost: of child care, 3; of GRA, *10*, *46*, 93; of health care, 3, 102; of rent, 2

debt: national, *25*; student loan, 3
defined-benefit plan, *27*, 57; active, 34; benefit of, 73–74; freezing of, 56; GRA as, 65; inactive, 34; options for, 137n2; reliance on, 31; returns on, 36; taxes on, 32; withdrawal from, 32–36
defined-contribution plan, 9, 15–16, 57
Denmark, 86, 91–92

Department of Labor, U.S., *22*, 59
disability, 73–74; rates of, *38*

economy: in Australia, 85; growth rates of, 3; macro, 29; savings in, 36–37
elderly, *5*, 5–6
Employee Benefit Research Institute, 24
employees. *See* workers
employers: competition of, 58–59; concerns of, 99; contribution from, 52–53, 57–59; mandates for, *101*; pensions from, 15; requirements of, 57–58; role of, 102. *See also* labor force
Employment Benefit Research Institute, 128
Employment Retirement Income Security Act (ERISA), 57, 59, 86–87
endowments, *64*
ERISA. *See* Employment Retirement Income Security Act
expenses, *26*

federal deficit: impact on, 29, 69; neutrality of, *54*
federal legislation, 87
Federal Reserve, *22*

Treasury Department, U.S., 80, 90, 123–24
Trump administration, 87; supporters of, *97*

unemployment, *38–39*
University of Technology, Sydney, 37
Urban Institute, The, *53*
U.S., 1; age in, 2–3; coverage across, *131–33*; federal legislation, 87; financial concerns of, 94; GDP in, *26*, 36–37, 58; government of, 70; leadership of, 87; population in, 5; ranking of, 86; salaries in, *50*, 52–53, 106; state plans in, 110; venture capitals in, 37; workforce in, 15

venture capitals, 37
voluntary plans, 64–65

Wall Street, 70, 109
wealth gap, *25–26*, 37–39; closing of, 69

WEF. *See* World Economic Forum
welfare programs, 93
withdrawal: from defined-contribution plans, 32–36; option for, 32
women. *See* workers
Work and Save, 126–27
workers: age of, 78–81; career length of, *38–39*, 127–29; challenges to, 2; concerns of, 94, 100; contribution from, 11–12, 52–56; futures of, 9; health of, *77*, 128; inequality for, 23; life expectancies of, 40; low-wage, 106; mandates for, 48; options for, 78; partnerships, 56; paths for, *76*; physical demand on, *38–39*; plan coverage for, *20*; poverty of, *25*; protection for, 70; self-employed, 56; Subchapter S corporations, 56. *See also* labor force
workforce, U.S., 15
World Economic Forum (WEF), 6–7, 44, 83
World War II, 91